FUNtastic
FR  **GS**™

Math
Volume 2

Grades K-2

Published by Ideal School Supply
an imprint of

Mc Graw Hill **Children's Publishing**

Authors: Jill Osofsky, Ann Roper
Editor: Karen Thompson

 Children's Publishing

Published by Ideal School Supply
An imprint of McGraw-Hill Children's Publishing
Copyright © 2004 McGraw-Hill Children's Publishing

Send all inquiries to:
McGraw-Hill Children's Publishing
3195 Wilson Drive NW
Grand Rapids, Michigan 49544

Funtastic Frogs™ Math Volume 2—grades K-2
ISBN: 0-7424-2771-4

1 2 3 4 5 6 7 8 9 MAL 09 08 07 06 05 04

The McGraw·Hill Companies

Table of Contents

About This Book

This book is one in a series of books designed to develop children's mathematical thinking and problem solving abilities. Each book supports the use of *Funtastic Frogs™* Counters in activities that teach key concepts.

Funtastic Frogs™ Counters are available in six different colors: green, blue, yellow, green, red, and orange; and in three sizes: 3 grams, 6 grams, and 12 grams. A unique lacing feature allows children to use the frogs in a wide range of counting and patterning activities.

As children use and manipulate the fun-to-hold *Funtastic Frogs™* Counters and along with the reproducible activities in this book, they will explore units in Addition and Subtraction, Fast Facts, Beginning Multiplication and Division, Making Graphs, and Beginning Problem Solving. Each unit is numbered and labeled throughout and is ideal for handy reference by busy teachers. Each separate unit focuses on a specific skill. There are Teacher's Notes for each unit that includes a list of materials, mathematical content, a skills chart, extensions, and investigations. Also find Sample Solutions, Activity Guides, and Reproducible Photocopy Master Pages.

Use this book and all the books in the series to extend and enrich your math program. These excellent resources are perfect additions to your classrooms to be used for learning centers, for large and small cooperative groups, or for individual and independent discovery. This book is excellent for home schooling, as well as anyone interested in helping young students get a head start in math. All the books support the recommendations as stated in the *NCTM Standards*.

Funtastic Frogs™ activity books and *Funtastic Frogs™* Counters and *Logs™* are available from Ideal School Supply, any Ideal School Supply Dealer, or our website at www.MHteachers.com.

FUNtastic FROGS™

Addition & Subtraction

Unit I

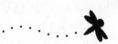

Teacher's Notes for This Unit

In Unit I, *Addition and Subtraction,* children use the frog counters to:

- count on to add
- combine groups to add
- write addition sentences
- take away to subtract
- write subtraction sentences
- understand the meaning of addition and subtraction
- learn the vocabulary for addition and subtraction

The activities in this unit are designed to teach higher level process skills in addition and subtraction using concrete objects. Children use the frog counters to act out situations that require combining groups to add or taking away parts of a larger group to subtract. They begin to connect the action of adding or subtracting to the words and symbols used to for the operations. All the activities support current mathematics standards.

Contents

This unit contains 24 activities divided into sections. Each section contains similar activities, giving the children the opportunity to practice and use each skill.

Sample solutions are provided on page 11. A photocopy master for the frog counters is included on page 12.

Math Skills and Understandings	Related Activities
Understand the meaning of addition and subtraction	Activities 1–24
Count on to add	Activities 1–5
Combine groups to add	Activities 6–15
Write addition sentences	Activities 11–15
Take away to subtract	Activities 16–19
Write subtraction sentences	Activities 20–24
Understand the vocabulary used for addition and subtraction	Activities 1–24

Suggestions for Classroom Use

Encourage children to share their thinking with the whole class. Talking about their thinking and discoveries helps them clarify their thoughts and allows others to hear how they might solve the same problem a different way. Talking about how they solve problems helps children make mathematical connections and deepens their understanding.

As children explore and manipulate the counters in a hands-on fashion, they gain confidence in their ability to make connections and to find creative ways to solve a problem. Students should have as many opportunities to experiment and manipulate the materials to formulate solutions.

Materials

You may wish to make an overhead transparency of the first activity page in each section as an introduction to the activities that follow.

For each child, pair of children, or group, you will need:
- pencils
- crayons or colored markers to match the colors of the frogs
- a tub of frogs in three sizes and six colors
- an activity sheet for each child or pair of children

If children are not able to record by writing numbers and coloring, make copies of page 12. The children can color and cut out the frogs, then paste or glue them in place to record.

Introducing the Activities

Encourage children to compare the frogs and tell how they are alike and how they are different. Ask them to describe the sizes and the different weights. Ask questions to probe their thinking such as: *Can you show me five frogs? Can you show me five another way? Can you tell me how many large frogs you have? Do you have more small frogs or medium frogs?*

When you introduce the activities in a section, lead the children through the first activity in that section. Discuss the directions and how to record their work. When reviewing the activity as a group, encourage children to talk about their discoveries. Make connections between the actions used for addition or subtraction and similar situations in the real world. Have children talk about their own experiences combining groups of objects, such as adding a new book or toy to a collection or their experiences taking away items from a larger number, such as taking one or two cookies away from a plate of six.

Mathematical Content

Activities 1–5: Count on by one, two, or three. Children match and count the frogs on the page. They add one, two, or three frogs and count on to find how many in all. As you discuss the activities, emphasize the language used for the actions. To reinforce the concepts, encourage pairs to make up stories or other scenes using similar numbers and actions. They can exchange problems with a different pair and solve that problem by counting on.

Activities 6–10: Combine groups for sums to 10. Children match frogs to make two groups then combine the groups to find how many in all. Emphasize the language used for the actions. As reinforcement, students working in pairs can make up situations and stories to act out using similar number groups.

Activities 11–15: Use numbers and symbols to write simple addition sentences. Children learn to use the symbols for addition to write simple addition sentences.

Activities 16–19: Take away to subtract. Children take away or separate frog counters from the whole group to act out subtraction of numbers through ten. As they perform the actions, supply the vocabulary used to describe the actions for subtracting. Children can make up similar situations or scenes to act out subtracting for the basic facts through ten.

Activities 20–24: Use numbers and symbols to write simple subtraction sentences. Children learn to use the symbols for subtraction and write simple subtraction sentences.

Sample Solutions for This Unit

These are sample solutions. Additional solutions are possible for some activities.

Activity

1 10
2 12

3A. 5, 6
3B. 7, 8

4A. 4, 6
4B. 6, 8

5A. 6, 9
5B. 8, 11

6A. 3
6B. 2
6C. 5

7A. 2
7B. 4
7C. 6

8A. 4
8B. 3
8C. 7

9A. 3
9B. 5
9C. 8

10A. 5
10B. 4
10C. 9

11A. 2+2=4
11B. 3+1=4
11C. 1+3=4

12A. 3+2=5
12B. 4+1=5
12C. 2+3=5

13A. 2+4=6
13B. 3+3=6
13C. 4+2=6

Activity

14A. 4+3=7
14B. 5+2=7
14C. 3+4=7

15A. 5+3=8
15B. 2+6=8
15C. 3+5=8

16A. 2
16B. 2
16C. Answers will vary.

17A. 2
17B. 3
17C. Answers will vary.

18A. 4
18B. 7
18C. Answers will vary.

19A. 4
19B. 2
19C. Answers will vary.

20A. 7−1=6
20B. 5−2=3
20C. Answers will vary.

21A. 6−2=4
21B. 10−2=8
21C. Answers will vary.

22A. 9−6=3
22B. 8−4=4
22C. Answers will vary.

23A. 10−5=5
23B. 9−4=5
23C. Answers will vary.

24A. 9−8=1
24B. 10−10=0
24C. Answers will vary.

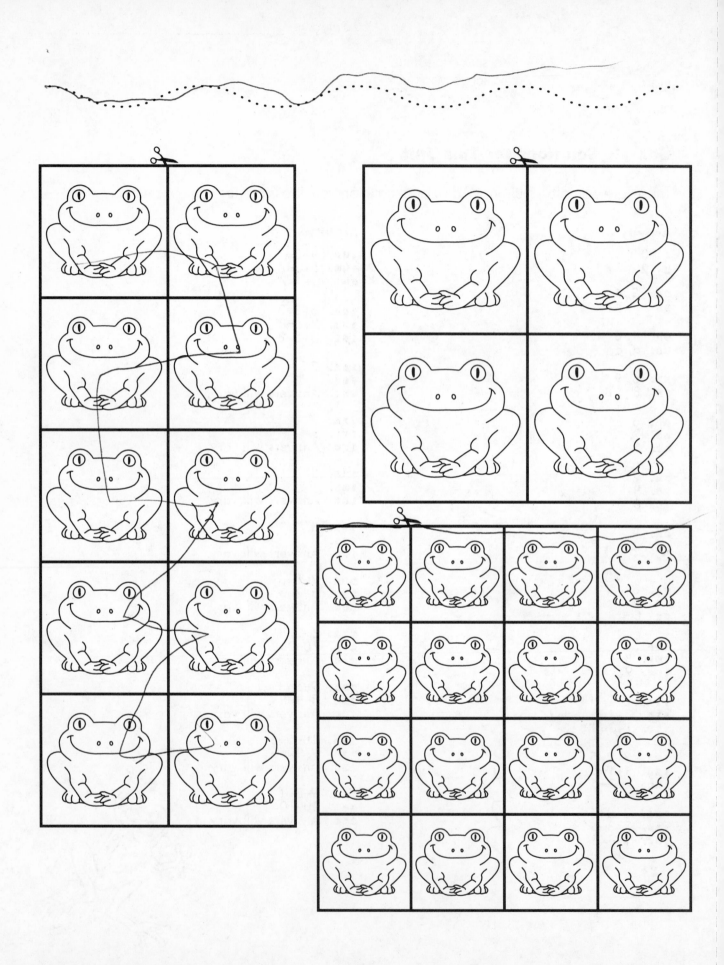

12

Name JOCK W.

Use small, medium, and large frogs
Record your work.

Match each frog.
Count.

How many frogs in all? 10 _____

ACTIVITY 2

Use small, medium, and large frogs. Record your work.

Name _____

Match each frog.
Count.

How many frogs in all? ___12___

Use small frogs.
Record your work.

Name _____

Match each frog.

A.

Count.
How many frogs? _5_

Add one more frog.
Count on.
How many in all? _____

B.

Count.
How many frogs? _8_

Add one more frog.
Count on.
How many in all? _12_

Use small and medium frogs. Record your work.

Name _____

Match each frog.

A.

Count.
How many frogs?_____

Add two more frogs.
Count on.
How many in all?_____

B.

Count.
How many frogs?_____

Add two more frogs.
Count on.
How many in all?_____

Use small frogs.
Record your work.

Name _____

Match each frog.

A.

Count.
How many frogs?_____

Add three more frogs.
Count on.
How many in all?_____

B.

Count.
How many frogs?_____

Add three more frogs.
Count on.
How many in all?_____

Use small and medium frogs
Record your work.

Name _____

Match each frog.
Count.

A.

How many frogs?_____

B.

How many frogs?_____

C. Put all the frogs together.
Count.

How many frogs in all?_____

0-7424-2771-4 Funtastic Frogs™ Math Volume 2

Use small and
medium frogs.
Record your work.

Name _____

Match each frog.
Count.

A.

B.

How many frogs?_____   How many frogs?_____

C. Put all the frogs together.
Count.

How many frogs in all?_____

Use small frogs.
Record your work.

Name _____

Match each frog.
Count.

A.

B.

How many frogs?_____   How many frogs?_____

C. Put all the frogs together.
Count.

How many frogs in all?_____

Use small frogs.
Record your work.

Name _____

Match each frog.
Count.

A.

B.

How many frogs? _____   How many frogs? _____

c. Put all the frogs together.
Count.

How many frogs in all? _____

Combine groups to add

ACTIVITY 10

Use small frogs.
Record your work.

Name _____

Match each frog.
Count.

A.    **B.**

How many frogs? _____   How many frogs? _____

c. Put all the frogs together.
Count.

How many frogs in all? _____

ACTIVITY 11

Name _____

Use small frogs.
Record your work.

A. Put 2 frogs on the  .

Put 2 frogs on the 🪵 .

Count how many frogs in all.
Write the addition sentence.

☐ + ☐ = ☐

B. Put 3 frogs on the 🪵 .

Put 1 frog on the 🪵 .

Count how many frogs in all.
Write the addition sentence.

☐ + ☐ = ☐

C. Use frogs to show 4 a different way.
Write the addition sentence.

☐ + ☐ = 4

Name _____

Use small frogs.
Record your work.

A. Put 3 frogs on the 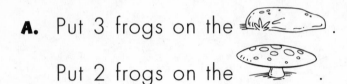 .

Put 2 frogs on the .

Count how many frogs in all.
Write the addition sentence.

$\boxed{}$ **+** $\boxed{}$ **=** $\boxed{}$

B. Put 4 frogs on the 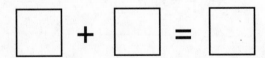 .

Put 1 frog on the  .

Count how many frogs in all.
Write the addition sentence.

$\boxed{}$ **+** $\boxed{}$ **=** $\boxed{}$

C. Use frogs to show 5 a different way.
Write the addition sentence.

$\boxed{}$ **+** $\boxed{}$ **=** $\boxed{}$

Name _____

Use small frogs.
Record your work.

A. Put 2 frogs on the 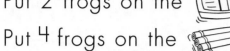 .

Put 4 frogs on the  .

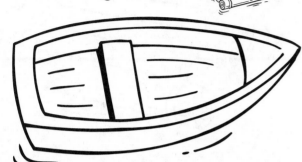 

Count how many frogs in all.
Write the addition sentence.

☐ + ☐ = ☐

B. Put 3 frogs on the 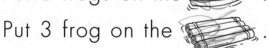 .

Put 3 frog on the  .

Count how many frogs in all.
Write the addition sentence.

☐ + ☐ = ☐

C. Use frogs to show 6 a different way.
Write the addition sentence.

☐ + ☐ = ☐

Use small frogs.
Record your work.

Name _____

A. Put 4 frogs on the  .

Put 3 frogs on the 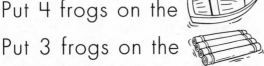 .

Count how many frogs in all.
Write the addition sentence.

☐ + ☐ = ☐

B. Put 5 frogs on the .

Put 2 frog on the .

Count how many frogs in all.
Write the addition sentence.

☐ + ☐ = ☐

C. Use frogs to show 7 a different way.
Write the addition sentence.

☐ + ☐ = ☐

Name _____

Use small frogs.
Record your work.

A. Put 5 frogs on the 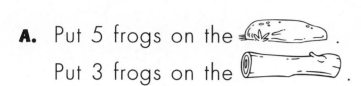 .

Put 3 frogs on the _____ .

Count how many frogs in all.
Write the addition sentence.

☐ + ☐ = ☐

B. Put 2 frogs on the  .

Put 6 frogs on the _____ .

Count how many frogs in all.
Write the addition sentence.

☐ + ☐ = ☐

C. Use frogs to show 8 a different way.
Write the addition sentence.

☐ + ☐ = ☐

Use small frogs.
Record your work.

Name _____

Use frogs.
Act out each story.

A. There are 4 frogs on the ⬚ .
2 frogs hop away.
How many frogs are left on the ⬚ ? _____

B. There are 5 frogs on the ⬚ .
3 frogs hop away.
How many frogs are left on the ⬚ ? _____

Make up your own story.

C. There are _____ frogs on the ⬚ .

_____ frogs hop away.

How many frogs are left on the ⬚ ? _____

Use small frogs.
Record your work.

Name _____

Use frogs.
Act out each story.

A. There are 6 frogs on the ⌐‾‾‾⌐ .
4 frogs hop away.
How many frogs are left on the ⌐‾‾‾⌐ ? _____

B. There are 8 frogs on the ⌐‾‾‾⌐ .
5 frogs hop away.
How many frogs are left on the ⌐‾‾‾⌐ ? _____

Make up your own story.

C. There are _____ frogs on the ⌐‾‾‾⌐ .

_____ frogs hop away.

How many frogs are left on the ⌐‾‾‾⌐ ? _____

Name _____

Use small frogs.
Record your work.

Use frogs.
Act out each story.

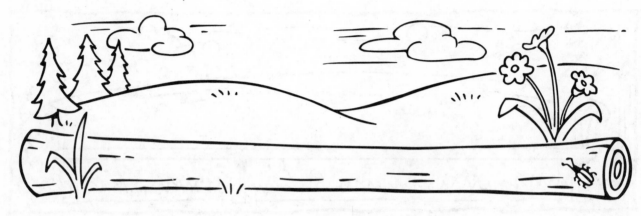

A. There are 7 frogs on the 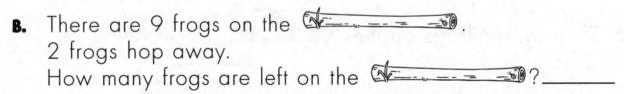.
3 frogs hop away.
How many frogs are left on the _____ ? _____

B. There are 9 frogs on the _____.
2 frogs hop away.
How many frogs are left on the _____ ? _____

Make up your own story.

C. There are _____ frogs on the _____.

_____ frogs hop away.

How many frogs are left on the  ? _____

**Use small frogs.
Record your work.**

Name _____

Use frogs.
Act out each story.

A. There are 9 frogs on the ~~~~~~~~~~ .
Take away 5 frogs.
How many frogs are left on the ~~~~~~~~~~ ? _____

B. There are 8 frogs on the ~~~~~~~~~~ .
Take away 6 frogs.
How many frogs are left on the ~~~~~~~~~~ ? _____

Make up your own story.

C. There are _____ frogs on the ~~~~~~~~~~ .

Take away _____ frogs.

How many frogs are left on the ~~~~~~~~~~ ? _____

31

Use small frogs.
Record your work.

Name _____

Use frogs. Act out each story.

A. There are 7 frogs on the 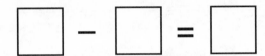 .
1 frog hops off.
How many frogs are left on the ? _____
Write the subtraction sentence.

☐ − ☐ = ☐

B. There are 5 frogs on the .
2 frogs hop off.
How many frogs are left on the ? _____
Write the subtraction sentence.

☐ − ☐ = ☐

Make up your own story.

C. There are _____ frogs on the .

_____ frogs hop off?

How many frogs are left on ? _____
Write the subtraction sentence.

☐ − ☐ = ☐

Use small frogs
Record your work.

Name _____

Use frogs. Act out each story. Write the subtraction sentence.

A. There are 6 frogs in the  .
2 frogs hop out.
How many frogs are left in the  ?_____

□ – □ = □

B. There are 10 frogs in the  .
2 frogs hop out.
How many frogs are left in the  ?_____

□ – □ = □

Make up your own story.

C. There are_____frogs in the  .

_____frogs hop out.
How many frogs are left in the  ?_____

□ – □ = □

0-7424-2771-4 *Funtastic Frogs™ Math Volume 2*

Use small frogs.
Record your work.

Name _____

Use frogs. Act out each story. Write the subtraction sentence.

A. There are 9 frogs in the  .
3 frogs hop out.
How many frogs are left in the 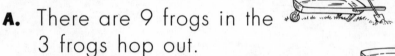 ? _____

☐ − ☐ = ☐

B. There are 8 frogs in the 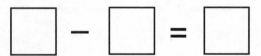 .
4 frogs hop out.
How many frogs are left in the 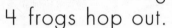 ? _____

☐ − ☐ = ☐

Make up your own story.

C. There are _____ frogs in the  .

_____ frogs hop out.

How many frogs are left in the 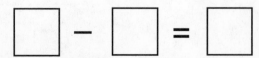 ? _____

☐ − ☐ = ☐

0-7424-2771-4 Funtastic Frogs™ Math Volume 2

ACTIVITY 23

Use small frogs.
Record your work.

Name _____

Use frogs. Act out each story. Write the subtraction sentence.

A. There are 10 frogs on the _____ .
5 frogs hop off.
How many frogs are left on the _____ ? _____

☐ − ☐ = ☐

B. There are 9 frogs on the _____ .
4 frogs hop off.
How many frogs are left on the _____ ? _____

☐ − ☐ = ☐

Make up your own story.

C. There are _____ frogs on the _____ .

_____ frogs hop off.

How many frogs are left on the _____ ? _____

☐ − ☐ = ☐

ACTIVITY 24

Use small frogs.
Record your work.

Name _____

Use frogs. Act out each story. Write the subtraction sentence.

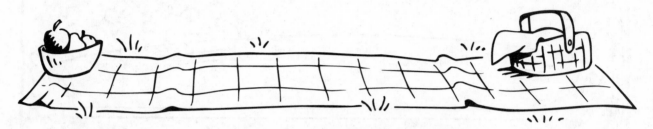

A. There are 9 frogs on the  .
8 frogs hop off.
How many frogs are left on the ____ ? _____

☐ − ☐ = ☐

B. There are 10 frogs on the ____ .
10 frogs hop off.
How many frogs are left on the ____ ? _____

☐ − ☐ = ☐

Make up your own story.

C. There are _____ frogs on the ____ .

_____ frogs hop off.

How many frogs are left on the  ? _____

☐ − ☐ = ☐

FUNtastic FROGS™

Fast Facts

Unit II

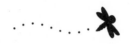

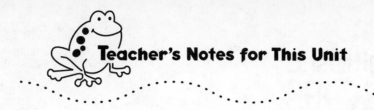

Teacher's Notes for This Unit

In Unit II, *Fast Facts,* children use the frog counters to:
- learn how to compute mentally
- learn strategies for remembering facts

The activities in this unit are designed to teach strategies for mental computation of addition and subtraction. These strategies should be taught after children have learned addition and subtraction, but before they have mastered the facts. Each strategy is introduced using frog counters to teach a way of thinking how to use numbers to find sums and differences quickly and correctly. The strategies utilize numbers with specific properties of addition and subtraction in ways that make sense to a child. Many of the activity pages are purposely designed to be open-ended and may be customized for practice of facts that children find most challenging.

The strategies facilitate memorization of over 100 addition facts. The subtraction strategies cover 64 subtraction facts. The activities in this book support current mathematics standards.

Contents
This unit includes 22 activities divided into sections for each strategy. Each section provides activities to practice each strategy in multiple ways. Suggestions for additional practice of the strategies are included.

Math Skills and Understandings	Related Activities
Count-on One, Two, and Add Zero	Activities 1–6
Add Doubles and Doubles-Plus-One	Activities 7–13
Make-a-Ten	Activities 14–16
Count Back to Subtract	Activities 17–22

Suggestions for Classroom Use

In discussions, encourage children to share their thinking with the whole class. Hearing about different ways to find a sum or difference helps children think about numbers flexibly. It gives them another option to consider when looking for a strategy to use to remember facts.

Materials

You may wish to make an overhead transparency of the first activity page for each strategy as an introduction to the activities that follow.

For each child, pair of children, or group, you will need:
- pencils
- crayons or colored markers to match the colors of the frog counters
- a tub of small frog counters
- an activity page for each child or pair of children

Note that for Activity 6 you will need a paper clip to be used as a spinner.

Introducing the Activities

When you introduce a strategy in a section, lead children through the first activity. Discuss the directions and how to record their work. When reviewing the activity, encourage the children to talk about the thinking they used when solving a problem. This will encourage others to explore different strategies and adopt the one that is most successful for their own use.

Since thinking of addition is a powerful strategy for finding subtraction facts, be sure children master all the addition facts before you introduce the subtraction strategies.

The strategies build on what is learned before, and should be done in sequence. When the children successfully find the facts using one strategy, it is time to introduce a new strategy. It is important to provide regular practice for the strategies that have been already learned. A variety of short meaningful practices will help children develop automatic recall of the facts. Suggestions for extending the practices for each strategy are included. Children must not only learn each strategy, they must practice it until they can recall it easily to find a fact quickly and correctly.

Mathematical Content by Section

Activities 1–6: Count-on one and two and add zero. The strategy is: Think, count-on one or two more to the larger number. Model the strategy in Activity 1 using five frogs. Ask: *How many frogs in the pond?* Add one more frog and ask: *What is one more than five? How can you think to find the sum?* Verbalize the thinking: Count-on one more to the larger number. Repeat using other numbers through ten. Introduce the strategy for counting-on two in a similar manner.

Demonstrate how to use a paper clip as a spinner for Activity 6. Bend one end of the paper clip out straight. With your pencil, hold the rounded end of the clip in the center of the spinner.

Most children quickly generalize that adding zero to any number does not change the number. However, since some children believe that any answer to addition must be larger, it is a good idea to practice this strategy. Introduce this strategy in the same manner as for counting-on one and two. Make up a story situation using zero as an addend and have children use the counters to act it out using Activity 5. Be sure to use zero as the first addend as well as the last addend in examples.

Activities 7–13: Add doubles and doubles-plus-one. These facts are the foundation for using other mental math strategies. Because both addends are the same, these facts are easy for children to memorize. Introduce the strategy using Activity 7. Ask: *How many frogs on the first log?* Have the children put the same number of frogs on the empty log, then ask: *How are the numbers alike? How many frogs in all?* Help them write the doubles number fact. Repeat the activity using different doubles facts. Pairs can finish the activity pages and continue acting out the facts through 10 + 10. Each child should record the doubles facts that require more practice.

Activities 8 and 9 provide visual images for recall. Many children will find them easier to remember because of the visual association for the fact. Distribute the activity pages and have children write the number fact for each picture.

Activity 10 invites the children to use the Daily Double Machine. Each number put in the machine is doubled and comes out the sum of the double.

Activity 11 introduces the doubles-plus-one strategy. Children can use frogs to model the related doubles fact then add one frog to model the doubles-plus-one fact. Work through two or three of the facts with the children. You might ask: *Who remembers the doubles strategy?* Call their attention to 2 + 3. Ask: *Which is the smaller number? Is there a way that I can change these numbers to make this a doubles fact?* If no one responds, use frogs to demonstrate how taking one frog from the group of three makes the doubles fact 2 + 2. Add one frog back to model the doubles-plus-one fact 2 + 2 + 1.

Children draw lines to connect matching doubles and doubles-plus-one facts on page 57. Pairs use two different colors of frogs to play the game on page 58, Doubles-Plus-One Tic-Tac-Toe. To place a frog counter on a Doubles-Plus-One square, a player must give the matching doubles fact. Children can self-check using the frog counters.

Activities 14–16: Make-a-ten. This strategy works for sums with addends of eight and nine. The ten-frame on page 59 works well for demonstrating the thinking for this strategy. Model the strategy using the 8 + 3 fact. Put eight frogs in the ten-frame, and three outside. Move two of the frogs from the outside to the inside of the ten-frame. Ask: *What fact do you see? How did I make this fact easy to remember?* Repeat using other addends with eight and nine. Guide children to observe that thinking of ten is an easier way to find the facts.

Activities 17–22: Counting back to subtract. This strategy works when a number can be easily subtracted mentally—usually numbers one or two. It is more challenging for children than the counting-on strategy for addition, and it should be done using the frogs, pictures, and numbers. Thirty-six facts can be mastered using this strategy. Demonstrate the strategy using the number line on page 62. Children must be able to find the larger number, identify the number or numbers that come before it, and count back to find the difference. Ask: *What is the larger number in the number sentence? What number comes before ten?* Use a frog counter to count back one on the number line. Ask: *How can I count back to find two numbers less than ten?* Have a child identify the larger number then count back two on the number line.

Use the game on page 67 to provide additional mental practice. Players use spinner A to find the subtrahend then use spinner B to find the minuend, 1 or 2. The player who spins must give the difference in a sentence. For example, *Seven is two less than nine.* The other player may use the frog counters or a calculator to check.

Suggestions for Additional Strategy Practice

It is important to provide a variety of short, meaningful practices to help children learn the strategies. Each strategy should be practiced using up to 10 activities so that the child can easily think of and use the strategy.

Oral Drill   To help children practice any strategy, give a weekly oral drill of up to ten facts. Ask fact questions that require using one of the strategies, such as: *What is two more than six? What is one more than nine? What is zero more than nine? What is double fours? What is five plus five?* Such questions ensure that the children practice the kind of thinking required for the strategy and fast recall of the facts.

Dice Drill   Make a set of dice labeled with numbers that correspond to the facts for the strategy to be practiced. Children roll the dice and add the numbers rolled. The player with the largest total after 10 rolls wins the game. Blank dice can be ordered from Ideal School Supply. You can also use self-adhesive stickers to customize the numbers on dice.

Dice for the counting-on strategy

Dice for the add zero strategy

Flash Cards: Counting-on   Prepare a set of cards with the numerals one through twenty. Write 1 more, 2 more, and 0 more on a second set of cards. Put each set of cards in separate stacks. To practice the counting-on one, two, or add zero strategy, children take turns picking a card from each pile and giving the sum. Players get to keep correct pairs of cards. This practice can be adapted to work for count back one or two to subtract. Prepare a different set of operation cards by writing 1 less and 2 less on cards.

Add Zero   Create sets of visual flashcards for practice. For example, show a 0-5 domino on one side and the corresponding number sentence on the other.

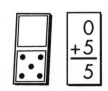

Doubles   Reinforce the visual thinking for the facts by preparing cards with pictures of double dominoes on them as well as the addition fact.

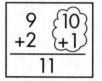

Make-a-Ten Make sets of flash cards showing the make-a-ten facts. Next to each fact show the corresponding ten-plus fact in a different color or circle in a bubble.

Lotto Games Make a lotto game board, a grid of four rows of four one-inch boxes.

To provide practice for the doubles strategy, distribute the lotto board to the entire class. Each child fills in the squares with sums of doubles. To play the game, call out such clues as double fours. If a child has the correct sum, a marker is placed on the number. The first player to get four in a row in any direction is the winner and becomes the next caller.

Doubles-plus-one can be practiced using the lotto board also. Write 12 near doubles facts in each square on the board. Make a corresponding set of near doubles flash cards for the game board. Children take turns taking a fact card and matching it to the corresponding near doubles sum on the game board. The first player to fill in the game board is the winner.

Make-a-Ten Lotto. Write the facts that can be found in the strategy in the boxes. Make a corresponding set of tens-plus flash cards. Children take turns picking a ten-plus fact card and matching it to the corresponding make-a-ten fact on the board. The first player to fill in the game board wins. Make-a-ten facts: 8 + 3, 3 + 8, 8 + 4, 4 + 8, 8 + 5, 5 + 8, 8 + 6, 6 + 8, 9 + 3, 3 + 9, 9 + 4, 4 + 9, 9 + 5 , 5 + 9, 9 + 6, 6 + 9, 9 + 7, 7 + 9.

The Ten-Frame. This frame helps children visualize the addition facts and subtraction facts.

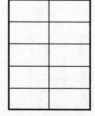

Sample Solutions for This Unit

Activity

1 5, 6 **DO MORE** 5+1=6

2A. 4, 8, 13
    6, 10, 15

2B. Number Count-on 1 sum

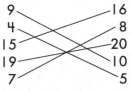

9   16
4   8
15   20
19   10
7   5

3 5, 7 **DO MORE** 5+2=7

4

IN	3	4	7	6	8	13	9	5
OUT	5	6	9	8	10	15	11	7

IN	9	7	1	5	4	2	6	14
OUT	11	9	3	7	6	4	8	16

5 Sums with addends of zero will vary.

6 Totals will vary. Emphasize using the count-on strategies.

7 3+3=6, 4+4=8, 5+5=10

8
$$\begin{array}{cccc} 1 & 2 & 3 & 4 \\ +1 & +2 & +3 & +4 \\ \hline 2 & 4 & 6 & 8 \end{array}$$

9
$$\begin{array}{cccc} 5 & 6 & 7 & 8 \\ +5 & +6 & +7 & +8 \\ \hline 10 & 12 & 14 & 16 \end{array}$$

10

IN	1	2	3	4	5	6
OUT	2	4	6	8	10	12

IN	7	8	9	10	4	5
OUT	14	16	18	20	8	10

Activity

11
1+1=2   4+5=9
2+2=4   1+2=3
3+3=6   2+3=5
4+4=8   3+4=7

12
5+5=10   8+9=17
6+6=12   9+10=19
7+7=14   5+6=11
8+8=16   6+7=13
9+9=18   7+8=15

13 Encourage students to use the doubles-plus-one strategy.

14 8+4=10+2=12
    5+8=3+10=13
    8+6=10+4=14
    7+8=5+10=15
    8+9=10+7 or
    7+10=17

15 9+5=10+4=14
    4+9=3+10=13
    9+7=10+6=16
    9+3=10+2=12
    8+9=10+7 or
    7+10=17

16

IN	8 + 3	4 + 8	5 + 8	8 + 6	7 + 8
OUT	10 + 1	10 + 2	10 + 3	10 + 4	10 + 5

IN	2 + 9	9 + 3	4 + 9	5 + 9	9 + 6
OUT	10 + 1	10 + 2	10 + 3	10 + 4	10 + 5

17 10−1=9
    17−1=16
    11−1=10
    15−1=14
    9−1=8
    14−1=13

18 12−1=11
    18−1=17
    16−1=15
    19−1=18
    20−1=19
    13−1=12

19 10−2=8
    11−2=9
    12−2=10
    15−2=13
    20−2=18
    18−2=16

20 8−3=5
    10−3=7
    11−3=8
    12−3=9
    15−3=12
    14−3=11

21A. 10−2=8

21B. 10−3=7

22 Totals will vary. Encourage students to use the count back strategy.

Use small frogs.

Name _____

Match the frogs.
Count.

How many frogs? _____
Add one more frog.
Think: Count-on one.

How many frogs in all? _____

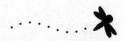

DO MORE
Write the number sentence.

☐ + ☐ = ☐

Name _____

A. Find each number on the log.
Think: Count-on one.
Write the number that is one more next to each number.

3 ____   7 ____   12 ____

5 ____   9 ____   14 ____

B. Look at each number.
Think: Count-on one.
Draw a line from each number to the count-on one sum.

Number	Count-on 1 sum
9	6
4	8
15	20
19	10
7	5

Use small frogs.

Name _____

Match the frogs.
Count.

How many frogs? _____
Add two more frogs.
Think: Count-on two.

How many frogs in all? _____

DO MORE

Write the number sentence.

☐ + ☐ = ☐

Name _____

When a number goes IN
the Count-on Two Machine,
it comes OUT two more.

Look at each IN number.
Write the missing OUT numbers.

IN	3	4	7	6	8	13	9	5
OUT	5	6	9					

IN	9	7	1	5	4	2	6	14
OUT	11	9	3					

DO MORE

Make a Count-on One Machine.
Make a table with IN numbers.
Let someone else write the OUT numbers.

Name _____

Match the frogs.
Count.

Some brave and fearless frogs,
Each wants to be a hero.
How many would there be,
If you simply added zero?

How many frogs? _____
Think: add zero

How many frogs in all? _____

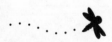

DO MORE

Write the number sentence.

☐ + ☐ = ☐

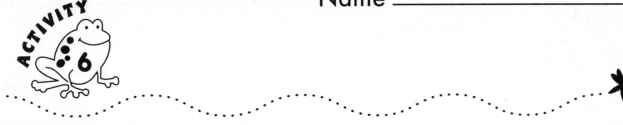

Name _____

Use Spinner A to get a number.
Use Spinner B. Count-on by that number.
Write the sum in the chart.

Each player finds 5 sums.
The player with the higher
total is the winner.

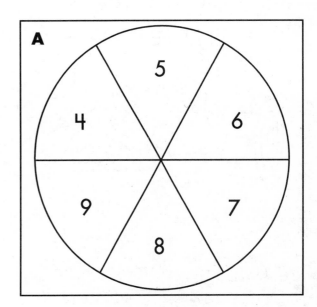

Player 1	Player 2
Total	Total

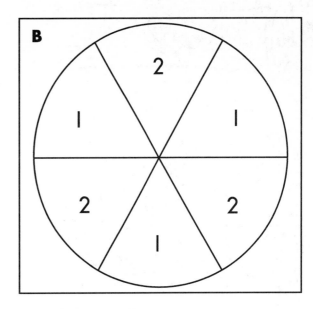

Use small frogs.

Name _____

Match the frogs on each log.
Count.
Put the same number of frogs on the empty log next to it.
How many frogs in all?
Write the number sentence for the doubles fact.

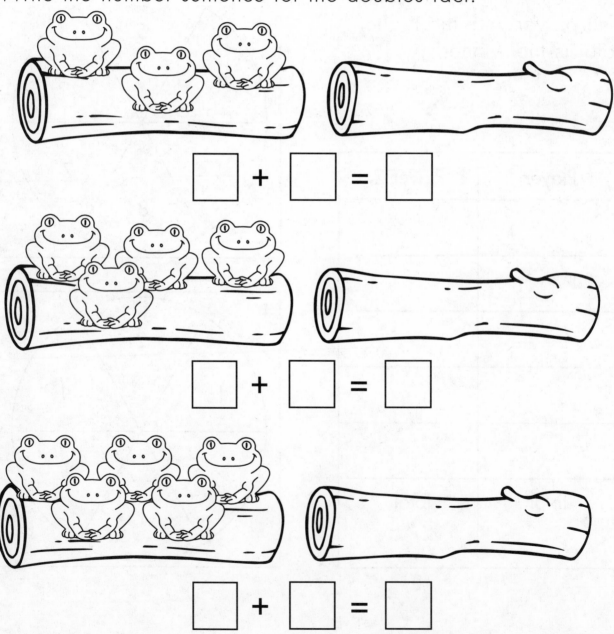

☐ + ☐ = ☐

☐ + ☐ = ☐

☐ + ☐ = ☐

Name _____

Look at the pictures.
Write the sum for each doubles fact.

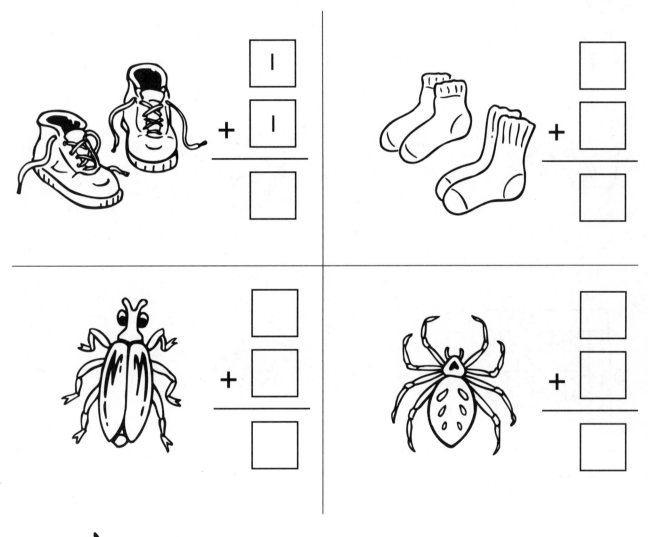

DO MORE

Make your own doubles fact pictures.
Write the doubles fact for each picture you make.

ACTIVITY 9

Name _____

Look at the pictures.
Write the sum for each doubles fact.

[hands picture]

$$\begin{array}{r} 5 \\ +\ 5 \\ \hline \square \end{array}$$

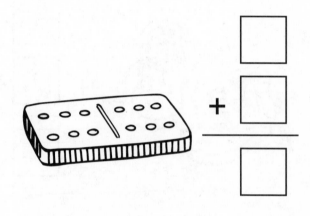

$$\begin{array}{r} \square \\ +\ \square \\ \hline \square \end{array}$$

[AUGUST calendar picture]

$$\begin{array}{r} \square \\ +\ \square \\ \hline \square \end{array}$$

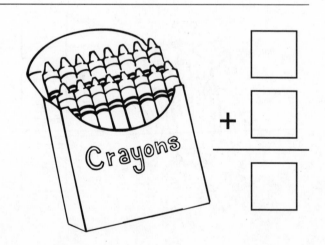

$$\begin{array}{r} \square \\ +\ \square \\ \hline \square \end{array}$$

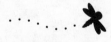

DO MORE

Make your own doubles fact pictures.
Write the doubles fact for each picture you make.

Name _____

When a number goes IN the Daily Double Machine,
it doubles and comes OUT
the sum of the double.

Think, double the number and find the sum.

Look at each IN number.
Write the missing OUT numbers.

IN	1	2	3	4	5	6
OUT	2	4	6			

IN	7	8	9	10	4	5
OUT	14	16	18			

DO MORE

Make your own Daily Double Machine. Make a table with
IN numbers. Let someone else write the OUT numbers.

Name _____

Use small frogs.

Use frogs to show each doubles fact.
Then add one frog to show each doubles-plus-one fact.
Draw lines to match each doubles fact to a doubles-plus-one fact.
Write the sums.

Doubles

$1 + 1 =$ ☐

$2 + 2 =$ ☐

$3 + 3 =$ ☐

$4 + 4 =$ ☐

Doubles-Plus-One

$4 + 5 =$ ☐

$1 + 2 =$ ☐

$2 + 3 =$ ☐

$3 + 4 =$ ☐

Double the smaller number and add one to find the sum.

Name _____

Draw lines to match each doubles fact to a doubles-plus-one fact.

Doubles

5 + 5 = ☐

6 + 6 = ☐

7 + 7 = ☐

8 + 8 = ☐

9 + 9 = ☐

Doubles-Plus-One

8 + 9 = ☐

9 + 10 = ☐

5 + 6 = ☐

6 + 7 = ☐

7 + 8 = ☐

> Double the smaller number and add one to find the sum.

0-7424-2771-4 Funtastic Frogs™ Math Volume 2

Use small frogs.

Name _____

Doubles-Plus-One Tic-Tac-Toe

Each player chooses a different color frog.

Take turns.

On your turn, put a frog on a doubles-plus-one fact.
Say the matching doubles fact. Then say the doubles-plus-one
fact. Example, if you put a frog on 1 + 2 say, "One plus one is
two. One plus one plus one is three."

You can use frogs to check your sum. If your sum is not correct,
take off your frog.

The first player to have three frogs in a row in any direction wins.

1 + 2	2 + 3	3 + 4
5 + 6	6 + 7	7 + 8
4 + 5	8 + 9	9 + 10

Name _____

Use small frogs.

When you want to add 8 to a number, think make-a-ten.

Example: 8 + 3 or 3 + 8
Put 8 frogs inside the ten-frame.
Put 3 frogs outside.
Move 2 frogs inside the frame to make a ten.
To find the sum, think 10 + 1. Say the sum.

Use frogs and the ten-frame.
Find the sums.

8 + 4 = ☐

5 + 8 = ☐

8 + 6 = ☐

7 + 8 = ☐

8 + 9 = ☐

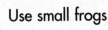

Name _____

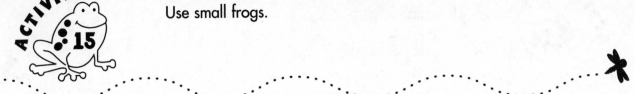

When you want to add 9 to a number, think make-a-ten.

Example: 2 + 9 or 9 + 2
Put 9 frogs inside the ten-frame.
Put 2 frogs outside.
Move 1 frog inside the frame to make a ten.
To find the sum, think 10 + 1. Say the sum.

Use frogs and the ten-frame.
Find the sums.

9 + 5 = ☐

4 + 9 = ☐

9 + 7 = ☐

9 + 3 = ☐

8 + 9 = ☐

Name _____

The Big Ten Machine changes facts.
Each fact that goes IN
comes OUT as a ten fact.

Look at each IN fact.
Write the missing OUT fact.

IN	8 + 3	4 + 8	5 + 8	8 + 6	7 + 8
OUT	10 + 1	10 + 2	10 + 3		

IN	2 + 9	9 + 3	4 + 9	5 + 9	9 + 6
OUT	10 + 1				

DO MORE

Make your own Big Ten Machine.
Make a table with some IN facts.
Let someone else write the OUT facts.

Use a small frog.

Count back to subtract.
Begin with the larger number.
Put a frog on that number.
Count back 1. Move the frog to that number.

The end number is the difference.
Write the difference.

8 9 10 11 12 13 14 15 16 17 18 19 20

Start at 10.
Count back 1.
Write the difference.

$\boxed{10} - \boxed{1} = \boxed{}$

Start at 17.
Count back 1.
Write the difference.

$\boxed{} - \boxed{} = \boxed{}$

Start at 11.
Count back 1.
Write the difference.

$\boxed{} - \boxed{} = \boxed{}$

Start at 15.
Count back 1.
Write the difference.

$\boxed{} - \boxed{} = \boxed{}$

Start at 9.
Count back 1.
Write the difference.

$\boxed{} - \boxed{} = \boxed{}$

Start at 14.
Count back 1.
Write the difference.

$\boxed{} - \boxed{} = \boxed{}$

Name _____

Use a small frog.

Count back to subtract.
Begin with the larger number.
Put a frog on that number.
Count back 1. Move the frog to that number.

The end number is the difference.
Write the difference.

<--•--•--•--•--•--•--•--•--•--•--•--•--•-->
   8   9 10 11 12 13 14 15 16 17 18 19 20

Start at 12.
Count back 1.
Write the difference.

| 12 | − | 1 | = | ☐ |

Start at 18.
Count back 1.
Write the difference.

☐ − ☐ = ☐

Start at 16.
Count back 1.
Write the difference.

☐ − ☐ = ☐

Start at 19.
Count back 1.
Write the difference.

☐ − ☐ = ☐

Start at 20.
Count back 1.
Write the difference.

☐ − ☐ = ☐

Start at 13.
Count back 1.
Write the difference.

☐ − ☐ = ☐

0-7424-2771-4 Funtastic Frogs™ Math Volume 2

ACTIVITY 19

Name _____

Use a small frog.

Count back to subtract.
Begin with the larger number.
Put a frog on that number.
Count back 2. Move the frog to that number.

The end number is the difference.
Write the difference.

←•——•——•——•——•——•——•——•——•——•——•——•——•→
  8   9 10 11 12 13 14 15 16 17 18 19 20

Start at 10.
Count back 2.
Write the difference.

$\boxed{10} - \boxed{2} = \boxed{}$

Start at 11.
Count back 2.
Write the difference.

$\boxed{} - \boxed{} = \boxed{}$

Start at 12.
Count back 2.
Write the difference.

$\boxed{} - \boxed{} = \boxed{}$

Start at 15.
Count back 2.
Write the difference.

$\boxed{} - \boxed{} = \boxed{}$

Start at 20.
Count back 2.
Write the difference.

$\boxed{} - \boxed{} = \boxed{}$

Start at 18.
Count back 2.
Write the difference.

$\boxed{} - \boxed{} = \boxed{}$

Use a small frog.

Name _____

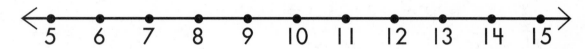

Count back to subtract.
Begin with the larger number.
Put a frog on that number.
Count back 3. Move the frog to that number.

The end number is the difference.
Write the difference.

5 6 7 8 9 10 11 12 13 14 15

Start at 8.
Count back 3.
Write the difference.

$\boxed{8}$ − $\boxed{3}$ = $\boxed{}$

Start at 10.
Count back 3.
Write the difference.

$\boxed{}$ − $\boxed{}$ = $\boxed{}$

Start at 11.
Count back 3.
Write the difference.

$\boxed{}$ − $\boxed{}$ = $\boxed{}$

Start at 12.
Count back 3.
Write the difference.

$\boxed{}$ − $\boxed{}$ = $\boxed{}$

Start at 15.
Count back 3.
Write the difference.

$\boxed{}$ − $\boxed{}$ = $\boxed{}$

Start at 14.
Count back 3.
Write the difference.

$\boxed{}$ − $\boxed{}$ = $\boxed{}$

ACTIVITY 21

Name _____

Use small frogs.

Use frogs to
act out the story.

A. 10 frogs were in the pond.
2 frogs hopped out to get a bug.

How many frogs are left?_____
Think: Count back 2.
Write the subtraction sentence.

B. 10 frogs were in the pond.
3 frogs hopped out to catch bugs.

How many frogs are left?_____
Think: Count back 3.
Write the subtraction sentence.

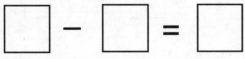

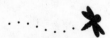

DO MORE

Make up your own frog story. Have a friend act it out.
Write the subtraction sentences.

     0-7424-2771-4 Funtastic Frogs™ Math Volume 2

ACTIVITY 22

Take turns.
Use spinner A to find a start number.
Use spinner B to find a count back number.

Say a sentence to give the difference.
Example: You spin a 7, then you spin −2.
Think: Count back 2 from 7 is 5.
Say, "Two from seven is five."

Write the difference in the chart.

Each player finds 5 differences.
The player with the lowest total
is the winner.

Player 1	Player 2
Total	Total

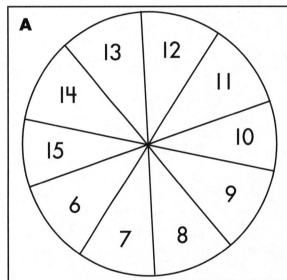

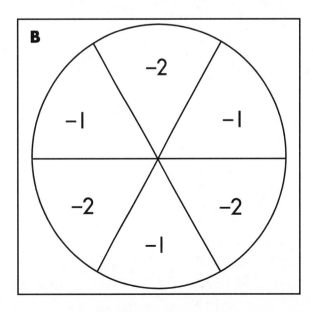

FUNtastic FROGS™

Beginning
Multiplication & Division

Unit III

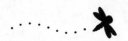

Teacher's Notes for This Unit

In Unit III, *Beginning Multiplication & Division,* children use the frog counters to:
* explore multiplication as repeated addition
* explore multiplication as addition of equal groups
* act out multiplication stories
* explore division as sharing
* explore division of groups

The activities in this unit are designed to develop readiness for multiplication and division. Children use the frog counters to act out the number relationships in multiplication and division. They use the counters to make equal groups and add them. They act out sharing a total number of counters among different groups to divide. These activities serve as a bridge in understanding between addition and multiplication and between subtraction and division, helping to develop readiness for more symbolic work with the operations in later years. All the activities support current mathematics standards.

Contents

This unit contains 22 activities divided into sections. Each section contains similar activities, giving the children the opportunity to practice and use each skill. Pairs of children can play the bingo game to practice the multiplication readiness skills introduced.

Solutions are provided on page 73. A photocopy master for the frog counters is also included on page 74.

Math Skills and Understandings	Related Activities
Use repeated addition to multiply	Activities 1–15; Game
Add equal groups to multiply	Activities 1–15; Game
Act out multiplication stories	Activities 6–10
Explore division as sharing and as making equal groups	Activities 16–22
Explore the meaning of multiplication	Activities 1–15; Game
Explore the meaning of division	Activities 16–22

Suggestions for Classroom Use

The activities are sequenced by level of difficulty within each section and from section to section. Modify a section if you find it is too challenging for your children, or not challenging enough.

The activities can be introduced to the whole class using an overhead projector, the chalkboard, or sitting in a circle on the floor. Once children understand the directions for the activities, they can work in pairs, small groups, or individually at a learning center.

Encourage children to share their thinking with the whole class. Talking about their thinking and discoveries helps children clarify their thoughts and allows others to hear how they might solve the same problem a different way. Talking about how they solve problems deepens their understanding and helps children make mathematical connections. Continued practice and repetition will increase confidence and subsequently, mastery.

Materials

You may wish to make an overhead transparency of the first activity page in each section as an introduction to the activities that follow.

For each child, pair of children, or group, you will need:
- pencils
- a tub of frogs in three sizes and six colors
- an activity sheet for each child or pair of children

Note that a pair of dice numbered 1–6 is needed for Frogs in a Row Bingo

Introducing the Activities

Encourage the children to describe the sizes and the different weights. Ask questions to probe their thinking such as: *Can you show a group of five frogs? Can you show two groups of four frogs? Do you have more groups of green frogs or groups of purple frogs?*

When you introduce the activities in a section, lead the children through the first activity in that section. Discuss the directions and how to record their work. When reviewing the activity as a group, encourage the children to talk about their thinking. Children will use a variety of methods to find an answer. They may count each frog, count on from a larger number, use skip counting, or use mental computation. Hearing different strategies to find an answer will provide models for other children to consider.

Make connections between the actions used in the activities and similar actions used in the real world. Have children talk about their own experiences adding equal groups to find a total, such as finding the total number of materials needed for a small group. Encourage them to talk about experiences sharing food or toy items among siblings or friends.

Mathematical Content by Section

Activities 1–5: Make and add equal groups. Ask children to use the frog counters to make groups of two. Have the children describe their groups, for example, three groups of two frogs. Tell the children to think of their groups and count how many in all. Ask for descriptions of the groups, for example, they might say there are three groups of two or I counted two, four, six frogs. Continue in the same way through Activity 5.

Activities 6–10: Act out multiplication stories. Children make equal groups of numbers, then add them to find how many in all. Discuss the stories that the children make up for the last activity.

Activities 11–15: Repeated addition. Children make rows of equal numbers and add to find how many in all. This is an introduction to using repeated addition to multiply.

Activities 16–22: Explore division. Before doing the activities, put the children into groups of four and give 20 frog counters to each group. Challenge the groups to find a way to share the counters equally. Ask: *How did you decide to share the frogs? How many frogs did each person get? Did everyone get the same number of frogs?* Discuss each activity using these types of questions to help children connect the actions they used to the process used in division of numbers.

Frogs in a Row Bingo. Children can play this game to reinforce the multiplication concepts introduced in the activities. Play a few rounds of the game with the children before they play independently. Players take turns rolling two dice numbered 1–6. After each roll, they use the numbers rolled to make rows of frogs. They choose one number and make that many rows of frogs. The other number tells them how many frogs to put in each row. Then they find how many frogs in all. If they have that number on their bingo card, they cover it with a frog. The first player to have four frogs in a row in any direction is the winner. If they don't have the number on their card, or if it's already covered, their turn is over.

Sample Solutions for This Unit

These are sample solutions. Additional solutions are possible for some activities.

Activity

1A. Two groups of two; 4 frogs in all
1B. Three groups of two; 6 frogs in all

2A. Three groups of three; 9 frogs in all
2B. Four groups of three; 12 frogs in all

3A. Two groups of four; 8 frogs in all
3B. Three groups of four; 12 frogs in all

4A. Two groups of five; 10 frogs in all
4B. Three groups of five; 15 frogs in all

5A. Five groups of two; 10 frogs in all
5B. Two groups of five; 10 frogs in all

6A. 4
6B. 10
6C. Answers will vary.

7A. 6
7B. 15
7C. Answers will vary.

8A. 8
8B. 12
8C. Answers will vary.

9A. 20
9B. 8
9C. Answers will vary.

10A. 10
10B. 25
10C. Answers will vary.

11A. Two frogs, 3 rows, 6 frogs in all
11B. Two frogs, 5 rows, 10 frogs in all
11C. Answers will vary.

12A. Five frogs, 2 rows, 10 frogs in all
12B. Five frogs, 4 rows, 20 frogs in all
12C. Answers will vary.

Activity

13A. Four frogs, 3 rows, 12 frogs in all
13B. Four frogs, 5 rows, 20 frogs in all
13C. Answers will vary.

14A. Three frogs, 3 rows, 9 frogs in all
14B. Three frogs, 4 rows, 12 frogs in all
14C. Answers will vary.

15A. Five frogs, 3 rows, 15 frogs in all
15B. Five frogs, 4 rows, 20 frogs in all
15C. Answers will vary.

16A. 3
16B. 4
16C. 5

17A. 2
17B. 3
17C. 4

18A. 3
18B. 4
18C. 5

19A. 3
19B. 4
19C. 5

20A. 5
20B. 3
20C. 5

21A. 2 frogs, 1 leftover
21B. 3 frogs, 1 leftover
21C. 4 frogs, 1 leftover

22A. 2 frogs, 1 leftover
22B. 3 frogs, 0 leftover
22C. 4 frogs, 2 leftover

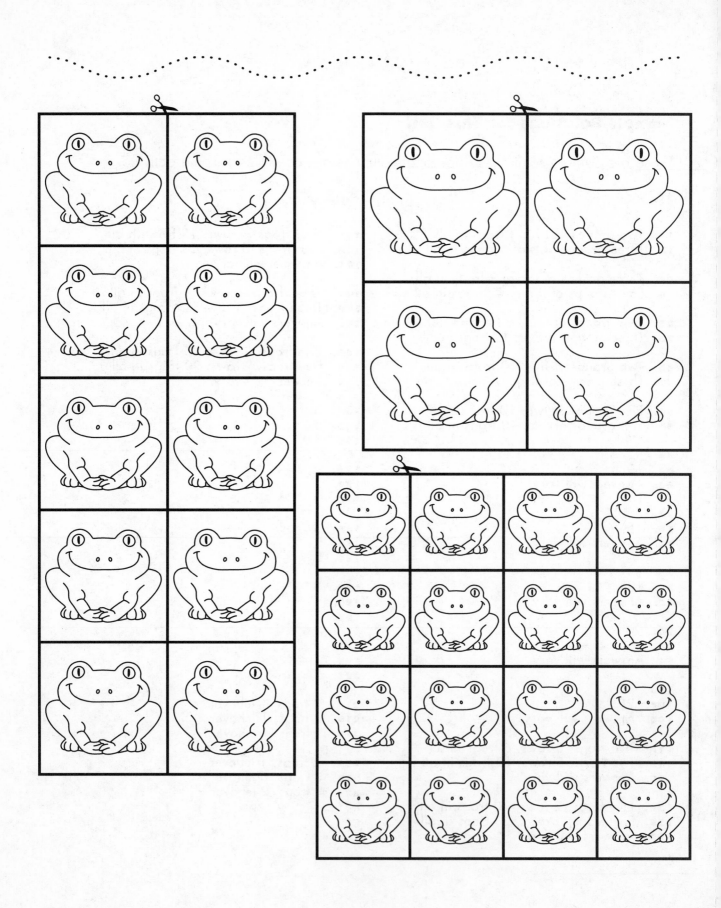

Name _____

Use small frogs.

A. Put 2 frogs on each puddle.

How many groups of 2?_____

How many frogs in all?_____

B. Put 2 frogs on each puddle.

 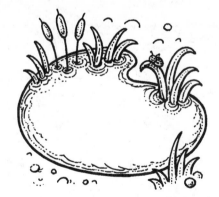 

How many groups of 2?_____

How many frogs in all?_____

Use small frogs

Name _____

A. Put 3 frogs on each lily pad.

How many groups of 3? _____

How many frogs in all? _____

B. Put 3 frogs on each lily pad.

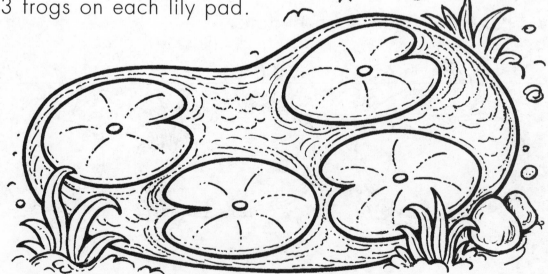

How many groups of 3? _____

How many frogs in all? _____

         0-7424-2771-4 Funtastic Frogs™ Math Volume 2

ACTIVITY 3

Name _____

Use small frogs.

A. Put 4 frogs on each log.

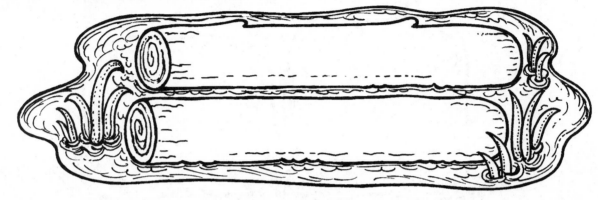

How many groups of 4?_____

How many frogs in all?_____

B. Put 4 frogs on each log.

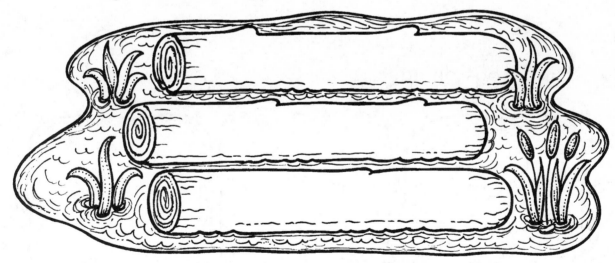

How many groups of 4?_____

How many frogs in all?_____

Use small frogs.

Name _____

A. Put 5 frogs on each rock.

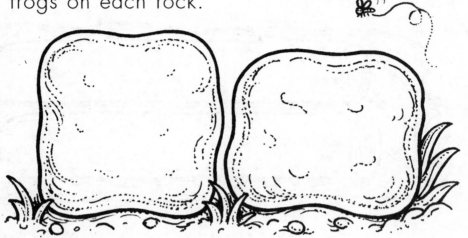

How many groups of 5? _____

How many frogs in all? _____

B. Put 5 frogs on each rock.

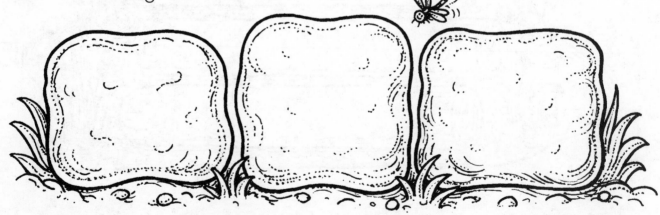

How many groups of 5? _____

How many frogs in all? _____

Use small frogs.

Name _____

A. Put 2 frogs on each mushroom.

How many groups of 2?_____

How many frogs in all?_____

B. Put 5 frogs on each lily pad.

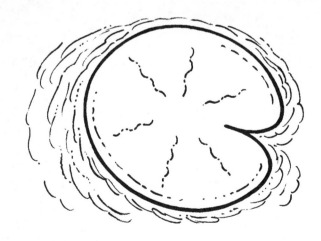 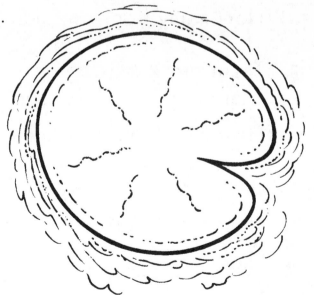

How many groups of 5?_____

How many frogs in all?_____

Use small frogs.

Name _____

Use frogs.
Act out each story.
Write the numbers.

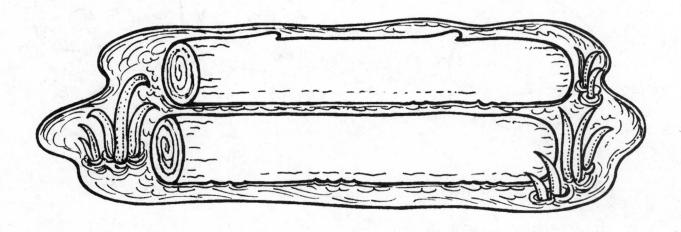

A. There are 2 logs.
There are 2 frogs on each log.

How many frogs are there in all? _____

B. There are 2 logs.
There are 5 frogs on each log.

How many frogs are there in all? _____

Make up your own story.

C. There are 2 logs.

There are _____ frogs on each log.

How many frogs are there in all? _____

Use small frogs.

Name _____

Use frogs.
Act out each story.
Write the numbers.

A. There are 3 tubes.
There are 2 frogs on each tube.

How many frogs are there in all?_____

B. There are 3 tubes.
There are 5 frogs on each tube.

How many frogs are there in all?_____

Make up your own story.

C. There are 3 tubes.

There are_____frogs on each tube.

How many frogs are there in all?_____

Use small frogs.

Name _____

Use frogs.
Act out each story.
Write the numbers.

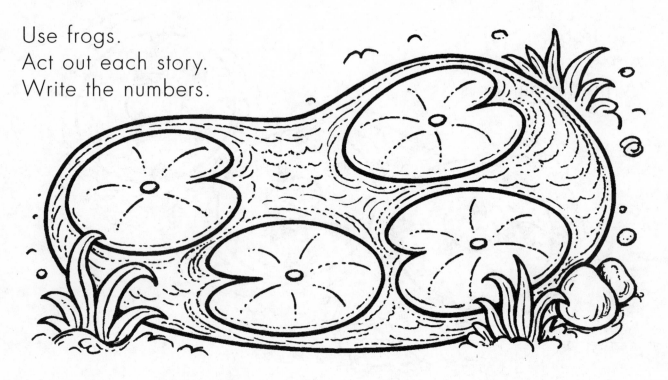

A. There are 4 lily pads.
There are 2 frogs on each lily pad.

How many frogs are there in all?_____

B. There are 4 lily pads.
There are 3 frogs on each lily pad.

How many frogs are there in all?_____

Make up your own story.

C. There are 4 lily pads.

There are_____frogs on each lily pad.

How many frogs are there in all?_____

ACTIVITY 9

Name _____

Use small frogs.

Use frogs.
Act out each story.
Write the numbers.

A. There are 4 tubes.
There are 5 frogs on each tube.

How many frogs are there in all? _____

B. There are 4 tubes.
There are 2 frogs on each tube.

How many frogs are there in all? _____

Make up your own story.

C. There are 4 tubes.

There are _____ frogs on each tube.

How many frogs are there in all? _____

         0-7424-2771-4 Funtastic Frogs™ Math Volume 2

Use small frogs.

Name _____

Use frogs. Act out each story. Write the numbers.

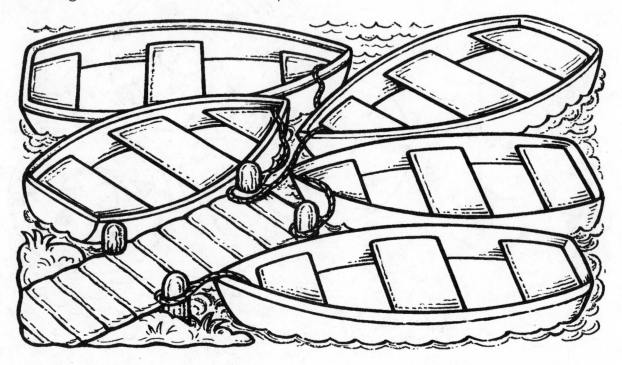

A. There are 5 boats.
There are 2 frogs in each boat.

How many frogs are there in all? _____

B. There are 5 boats.
There are 5 frogs in each boat.

How many frogs are there in all? _____

Make up your own story.

C. There are 5 boats.

There are _____ frogs in each boat.

How many frogs are there in all? _____

Use small frogs.

Name _____

A. Make 3 equal rows like the one above.

How many frogs are in each row?_____

How many rows are there?_____

How many frogs are there in all?_____

B. Make 5 equal rows like the one above.

How many frogs are in each row?_____

How many rows are there?_____

How many frogs are there in all?_____

C. Make your own number of equal rows.

How many frogs are in each row?_____

How many rows are there?_____

How many frogs are there in all?_____

Name _____

Use small frogs.

A. Make 2 equal rows like the one above.

How many frogs are in each row?_____

How many rows are there?_____

How many frogs are there in all?_____

B. Make 4 equal rows like the one above.

How many frogs are in each row?_____

How many rows are there?_____

How many frogs are there in all?_____

C. Make your own number of equal rows.

How many frogs are in each row?_____

How many rows are there?_____

How many frogs are there in all?_____

Name _____

Use small frogs.

A. Make 3 equal rows like the one above.

How many frogs are in each row?_____

How many rows are there?_____

How many frogs are there in all?_____

B. Make 5 equal rows like the one above.

How many frogs are in each row?_____

How many rows are there?_____

How many frogs are there in all?_____

C. Make your own number of equal rows.

How many frogs are in each row?_____

How many rows are there?_____

How many frogs are there in all?_____

Use small, medium, and large frogs.

Name _____

A. Make 3 equal rows like the one above.

How many frogs are in each row? _____

How many rows are there? _____

How many frogs are there in all? _____

B. Make 4 equal rows like the one above.

How many frogs are in each row? _____

How many rows are there? _____

How many frogs are there in all? _____

C. Make your own number of equal rows.

How many frogs are in each row? _____

How many rows are there? _____

How many frogs are there in all? _____

Use small, medium, and large frogs.

Name _____

A. Make 3 equal rows like the one above.

How many frogs are in each row? _____

How many rows are there? _____

How many frogs are there in all? _____

B. Make 4 equal rows like the one above.

How many frogs are in each row? _____

How many rows are there? _____

How many frogs are there in all? _____

C. Make your own number of equal rows.

How many frogs are in each row? _____

How many rows are there? _____

How many frogs are there in all? _____

Name _____

Use small frogs.

Act out each story.
Write the numbers.

A. 2 children want to
share 6 frogs.
Give each child the
same number of frogs.

How many frogs for each child?_____

B. 2 children want to share 8 frogs.
Give each child the same number of frogs.

How many frogs for each child?_____

C. 2 children want to share 10 frogs.
Give each child the same number of frogs.

How many frogs for each child?_____

Use small frogs.

Name _____

Act out each story.
Write the numbers.

A. 4 children want
to share 8 frogs.
Give each child
the same number of frogs.

How many frogs for each child?_____

B. 4 children want to share 12 frogs.
Give each child the same number of frogs.

How many frogs for each child?_____

C. 4 children want to share 16 frogs.
Give each child the same number of frogs.

How many frogs for each child?_____

Use small frogs.

Name _____

Act out each story.
Write the numbers.

A. 9 frogs want to
share 3 houses.
Put the same number
of frogs in each house.

How many frogs in each house?_____

B. 12 frogs want to share 3 houses.
Put the same number of frogs in each house.

How many frogs in each house?_____

C. 15 frogs want to share 3 houses.
Put the same number of frogs in each house.

How many frogs in each house?_____

Use small frogs.

Name _____

Act out each story. Write the numbers.

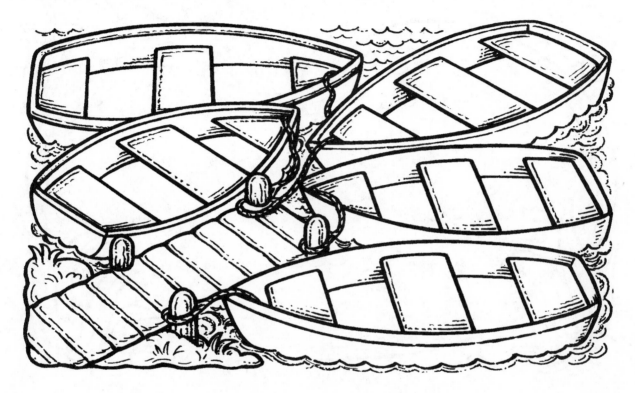

A. 15 frogs want to share 5 boats.
Put the same number of frogs on each boat.

How many frogs on each boat? _____

B. 20 frogs want to share 5 boats.
Put the same number of frogs on each boat.

How many frogs on each boat? _____

C. 25 frogs want to share 5 boats.
Put the same number of frogs on each boat.

How many frogs on each boat? _____

Name _____

Use small frogs.

Act out each story. Write the numbers.

A. 10 frogs want to swim in groups of 2.
Show the groups.

How many groups of 2?_____

B. 15 frogs want to swim in groups of 5.
Show the groups.

How many groups of 5?_____

C. 20 frogs want to swim in groups of 4.
Show the groups.

How many groups of 4?_____

Use small frogs.

Name _____

Act out each story.
Write the numbers.

A. 2 boys want to
share 5 frogs.
Give each boy the
same number of frogs.

How many frogs for each boy?_____

How many frogs leftover?_____

B. 2 girls want to share 7 frogs.
Give each girl the same number of frogs.

How many frogs for each girl?_____

How many frogs leftover?_____

C. 2 boys want to share 9 frogs.
Give each boy the same number of frogs.

How many frogs for each boy?_____

How many frogs leftover?_____

Use small frogs.

Name _____

Act out each story.
Write the numbers.

A. 7 frogs want to share 3 rafts.
Put the same number of frogs on each raft.

How many frogs on each raft?_____

How many frogs leftover?_____

B. 9 frogs want to share 3 rafts.
Put the same number of frogs on each raft.

How many frogs on each raft?_____

How many frogs leftover?_____

C. 14 frogs want to share 3 rafts.
Put the same number of frogs on each raft.

How many frogs on each raft?_____

How many frogs leftover?_____

Name _____

 **Frogs in a Row Bingo**

For 2 players

READY

You need one pair of dice numbered 1–6 and a tub of frogs.

SET

Each player takes a bingo card. Both players roll a die. The player who rolls the higher number begins the game.

PLAY

Take turns. On each turn, you will make rows of frogs. To do this, roll the dice. Choose one number. That number tells you how many rows of frogs to make. The other number tells you how many frogs to put in each row. Find how many frogs in all. If you have that number on your card, cover it with a frog. If you do not have the number or if there is a frog on it, your turn is over.

The first player to have 4 frogs in a row in any direction is the winner.

Name _____

Frogs in a Row Bingo

16	8	30	18
25	12	16	10
4	9	6	24
5	20	3	15

9	5	20	10
4	36	15	24
16	8	30	18
25	12	3	6

0-7424-2771-4 Funtastic Frogs™ Math Volume 2

FUNtastic
FR🐸GS™

Making Graphs

Unit IV

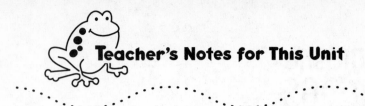

Teacher's Notes for This Unit

In Unit IV, *Making Graphs,* children use the frog counters to:
- sort and classify objects by color and size
- graph data using objects
- graph data using symbols
- analyze graphs to compare quantities

The activities in this unit are designed to help children learn how to graph data using objects, pictures, and symbols in a way that shows information clearly. The children are actively involved using the frog counters to make the graphs. They sort, classify, and graph the frog counters and talk about what the graph is about in a way that makes sense to them. They use the information in the graphs to compare quantities. The activities in this unit support current mathematics standards.

Contents
This unit contains 22 activities divided into sections. Each section contains similar activities, giving children the opportunity to apply and practice each skill.

Sample solutions are provided on page 104. A photocopy master for the frog counters is also included on page 105. Photocopy masters for two sizes of graphing paper are included on pages 106 and 107.

Math Skills and Understandings	Related Activities
Sort and classify objects	Activities 1–22
Collect and represent data	Activities 1–22
Use concrete objects to represent data	Activities 1–22
Display data using sorting diagrams	Activities 1–4
Display data using graphs	Activities 5–22
Analyze graphs to compare quantities	Activities 7–22

Suggestions for Classroom Use

Encourage children to share their thinking with the whole class. Talking about their thinking helps them clarify their thoughts and allows others to hear how they might solve the same problem a different way. Talking about how they solve problems helps children make mathematical connections and deepens their understanding.

Materials

You may wish to make an overhead transparency of the first activity page for each section as an introduction to the activities that follow.

For each pupil, pair of children, or group, you will need:
- pencils
- crayons or colored markers to match the colors of the frog counters
- a tub of small and medium frog counters in six colors
- an activity page for each child

Introducing the Activities

Introduce terms that appear in this unit, such as *sort, collect, represent, diagram, graph,* and *set* informally. Use the terms that are appropriate for your children's age level. It is also a good time to introduce the symbols that will appear on some of the activity pages. The frog sizes are referred to as *small* and *medium.* The color for each frog is represented by the first letter of each color on the chest of the frog. Be sure all pupils are familiar with these terms before you begin instruction.

When you introduce a section of the unit, lead the children through the first few activities in that section. Point out the need for a title, a label for the axis, and numbers on each graph. It is important that the whole class participate in making model graphs before constructing graphs in small groups. Discuss the directions and how to record their work.

Once a graph is completed, the most important activity is discussing what the graph represents. When reviewing an activity with the group, encourage the children to talk about their discoveries. Ask such questions as: *What does this graph tell us? Which row (column) has more (fewer) frogs? How many more (fewer)?* Talking about the graphs will help the children make connections between the making of the graph and the information it represents. As a whole group, experiment with graphing different attributes that the children possess. Some ideas to graph are family size, number of pets, and favorite books.

Mathematical Content by Section

Activities 1–4: Sorting by color and size. Use Activity 1 as an introduction to Activities 2–6. Have the children match the frogs and sort them by color, then sort them by size. Skills required making a graph include sorting and classifying. The activity pages review these skills.

Activities 5–6: Graphing color and size. Children sort frog counters by colors and sizes then graph, count, and compare the data. The vertical graphs in each activity begin at the bottom of the page and are built up. These activities provide children with a model of how to organize a graph. Point out the need for a title, a label for the axis, and numbers on the graph. Discuss each graph as a group, asking such questions as: *How many green frogs? Which group has more frogs? How many more?*

Activities 7–14: Organizing data using vertical graphs. Use Activity 7, **Frog Pond,** as an introduction to Activities 8-10. Have the children match the frogs then sort them by color. Use Activity 11, **Frog Park,** as an introduction to Activities 12–14. Have the children match the frogs then sort them by color. In Activities 8–14 children place frogs on the graphs to represent the data. Children color squares in the graph to record, then compare the number of frogs and discuss what the graphs represent.

Activities 15–22: Organizing data using horizontal graphs. Use Activity 15, **Frog House,** as an introduction to Activities 16–18. Have the children match the frogs then sort them by size and color. Use Activity 19, **Frog Town,** in the same way as introduction to Activities 20–22. The graphs in these activities are presented in a horizontal format so children learn that a graph can be constructed in more than one way. In Activities 16–22 children place frogs on the graphs to represent the data. They color squares in the graphs to record, then compare the number of frogs and discuss what the graphs represent.

Sample Solutions for This Unit

These are sample solutions. Additional solutions are possible for some activities.

Activity

1A. 3 green frogs
1B. 4 blue frogs

2A. 5 small frogs
2B. 3 medium frogs
2C. medium frogs
2D. 2

3A. 6 small yellow frogs
3B. 3 medium red frogs
3C. small yellow frogs
3D. 3

4A. 6 small purple frogs
4B. 2 medium orange frogs
4C. small purple frogs
4D. 4

5A. 2 small yellow frogs
5B. 4 small orange frogs
5C. orange frogs
5D. 2

6A. 5 red frogs
6B. 1 blue frog
6C. blue frogs
6D. 4

8A. 5 green frogs
8B. 3 yellow frogs
8C. green frogs
8D. 2

9A. 2 red frogs
9B. 4 blue frogs
9C. red frogs
9D. 2

10A. 2 orange frogs
10B. 5 purple frogs
10C. purple frogs
10D. 3

12A. 5 green frogs
12B. 4 yellow frogs
12C. 3 orange frogs
12D. green frogs
12E. orange frogs

Activity

13A. 3 orange frogs
13B. 4 purple frogs
13C. 2 blue frogs
13D. purple frogs
13E. blue frogs

14A. 2 blue frogs
14B. 5 green frogs
14C. 4 purple frogs
14D. green frogs
14E. blue frogs

16A. 5 small yellow frogs
16B. 4 medium orange frogs
16C. small yellow frogs
16D. 1

17A. 5 small green frogs
17B. 3 small purple frogs
17C. 4 medium orange frogs
17D. small green frogs
17E. small purple frogs

18A. 5 small yellow frogs
18B. 1 small blue frog
18C. 3 medium red frogs
18D. small yellow frogs
18E. small blue frogs

20A. 5 small green frogs
20B. 4 small orange frogs
20C. 2 medium green frogs
20D. small green frogs

21A. 5 small green frogs
21B. 2 medium green frogs
21C. small green frogs
21D. medium green frogs

22A. small green
22B. medium green
22C. small blue frogs and small yellow frogs

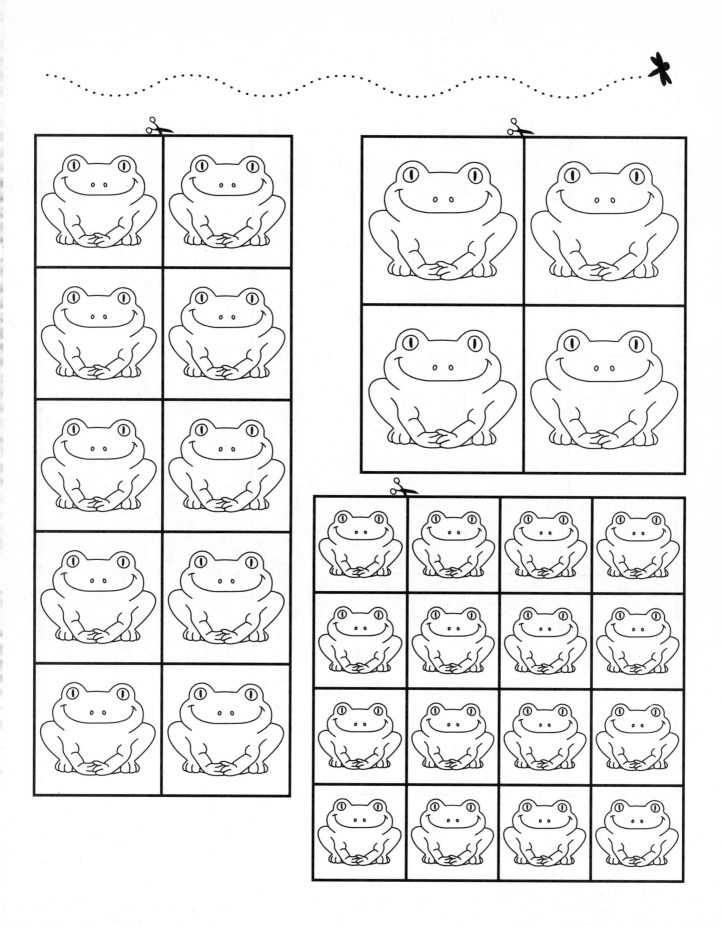

0-7424-2771-4 Funtastic Frogs™ Math Volume 2

106

 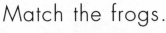

Use small frogs.
Record your work.

Name _____

Match the frogs.

Sort your frogs by color.
Put each frog where it belongs.

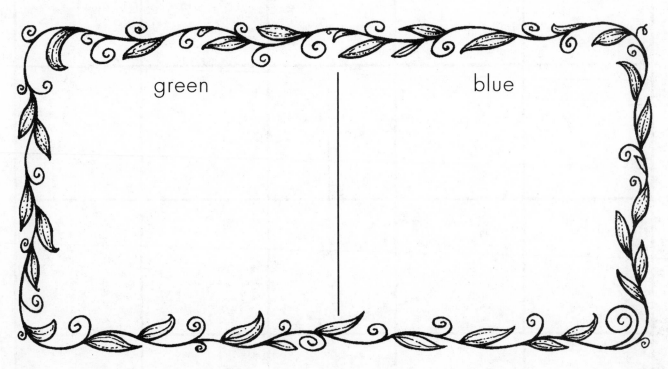

green   blue

A. How many green frogs? _____

B. How many blue frogs? _____

ACTIVITY 2

Use small and
medium frogs.
Record your work.

Name _____

Match the frogs.

Sort your frogs by size.
Put each frog where it belongs.

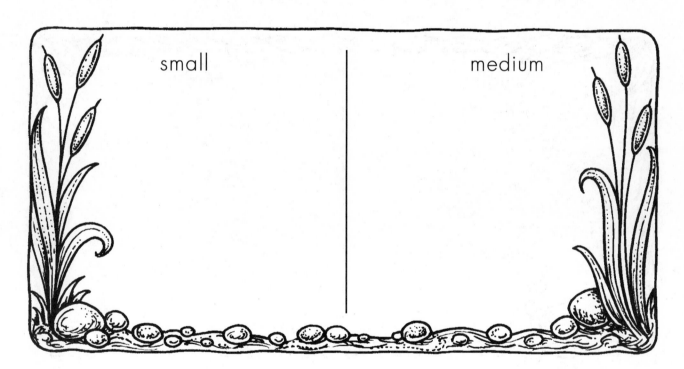

small   medium

A. How many small frogs? _____

B. How many medium frogs? _____

C. Which group has fewer frogs? _____

D. How many fewer frogs? _____

Use small and
medium frogs.
Record your work.

Match the frogs.

Sort your frogs by color and size.
Put each frog where it belongs.

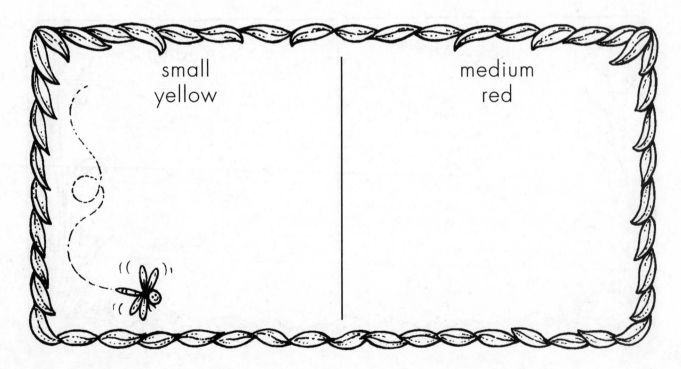

small yellow	medium red

A. How many small yellow frogs?_____

B. How many medium red frogs?_____

C. Which group has more frogs?_____

D. How many more frogs?_____

Name _____

Use small and
medium frogs.
Record your work.

Match the frogs.

Sort your frogs by color and size.
Put each frog where it belongs.

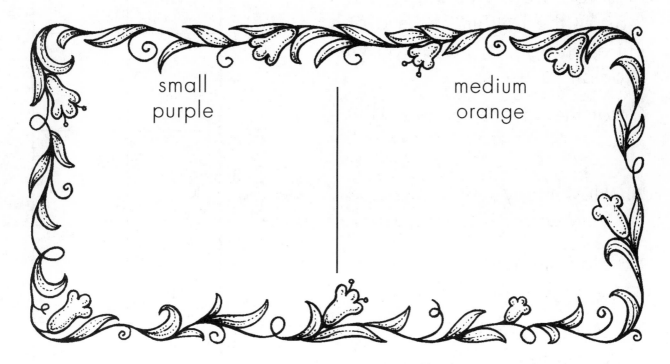

small
purple

medium
orange

A. How many small purple frogs?_____

B. How many medium orange frogs?_____

C. Which group has more frogs?_____

D. How many more frogs?_____

Use small frogs.
Record your work.

Name _____

Match the frogs.

Sort your frogs by color.
Start at the bottom of the graph.
Put each frog on the graph where it belongs.

Color the squares to record.

A. How many yellow frogs? _____

B. How many orange frogs? _____

C. Which group has more frogs? _____

D. How many more frogs? _____

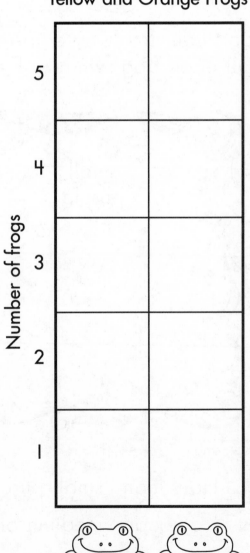

Yellow and Orange Frogs

ACTIVITY 6

Name _____

Use small frogs.
Record your work.

Match the frogs.

Red and Blue Frogs

Sort your frogs by color.
Start at the bottom of the graph.
Put each frog on the graph where it belongs.

Color the squares to record.

A. How many
red frogs? _____

B. How many
blue frogs? _____

C. Which group
has fewer frogs? _____

D. How many
fewer frogs? _____

Number of frogs

5
4
3
2
1

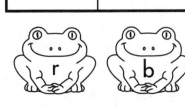

Name _____

Use small frogs.

Match the frogs.

Use Frog Pond
and small frogs.
Record your work.

Name _____

Match the frogs in Frog Pond.

Sort your frogs by color.
Start at the bottom of the graph.
Put each frog on the graph where it belongs.

Color the graph to record.

Frog Pond Frogs

A. How many
green frogs?_____

B. How many
yellow frogs?_____

C. Which group
has more frogs?_____

D. How many
more frogs?_____

Number of frogs

5

4

3

2

1

g   y

Use Frog Pond
and small frogs.
Record your work.

Name _____

Match the frogs in Frog Pond.

Sort your frogs by color.
Start at the bottom of the graph.
Put each frog on the graph where it belongs.

Color the graph to record.

A. How many
red frogs?_____

B. How many
blue frogs?_____

C. Which group
has fewer frogs?_____

D. How many
fewer frogs?_____

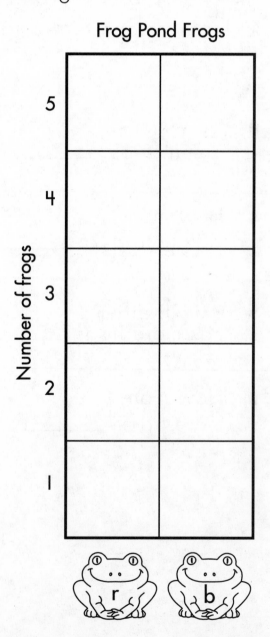

Frog Pond Frogs

Use Frog Pond
and small frogs.
Record your work.

Name _____

Match the frogs in Frog Pond.

Sort your frogs by color.
Start at the bottom of the graph.
Put each frog on the graph where it belongs.

Color the graph to record.

A. How many
orange frogs?_____

B. How many
purple frogs?_____

C. Which group
has more frogs?_____

D. How many
more frogs?_____

Frog Pond Frogs

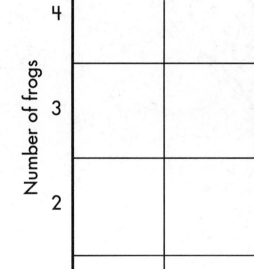

Name _____

Match the frogs.

ACTIVITY 12

Use Frog Park
and small frogs.
Record your work.

Name _____

Match the frogs in Frog Park.

Sort your frogs by color.
Start at the bottom of the graph.
Put each frog on the graph where it belongs.

Color the graph to record.

A. How many
green frogs? _____

B. How many
yellow frogs? _____

C. How many
orange frogs? _____

D. Which group has
the most frogs? _____

E. Which group has
the fewest frogs? _____

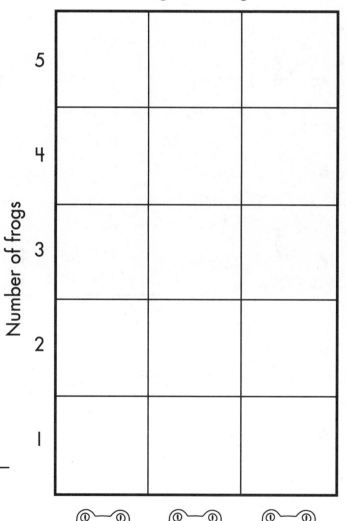

Frog Park Frogs

Use Frog Park
and small frogs.
Record your work.

Name _____

Match the frogs in Frog Park.

Sort your frogs by color.
Start at the bottom of the graph.
Put each frog on the graph where it belongs.

Color the graph to record.

Frog Park Frogs

A. How many
orange frogs?_____

B. How many
purple frogs?_____

C. How many
blue frogs?_____

D. Which group has
the most frogs?_____

E. Which group has
the fewest frogs?_____

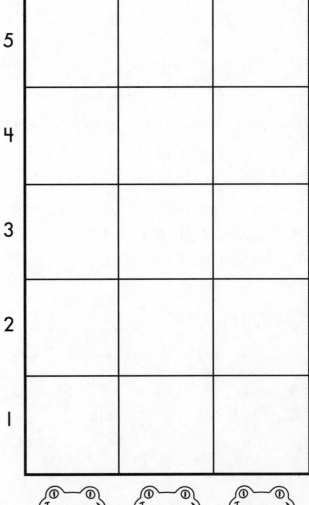

ACTIVITY 14

Use Frog Park
and small frogs.
Record your work.

Name _____

Match the frogs in Frog Park.

Sort your frogs by color.
Start at the bottom of the graph.
Put each frog on the graph where it belongs.

Color the graph to record.

A. How many
blue frogs? _____

B. How many
green frogs? _____

C. How many
purple frogs? _____

D. Which group has
the most frogs? _____

E. Which group has
the fewest frogs? _____

Frog Park Frogs

Number of frogs

5

4

3

2

1

Use small and
medium frogs.

Match the frogs.

Use Frog House and
small and medium frogs.
Record your work.

Name _____

Match the frogs in Frog House.
Sort your frogs by color and size.
Start at the left side of the graph.
Put each frog on the graph where it belongs.

Color the graph to record.

Frog House Frogs

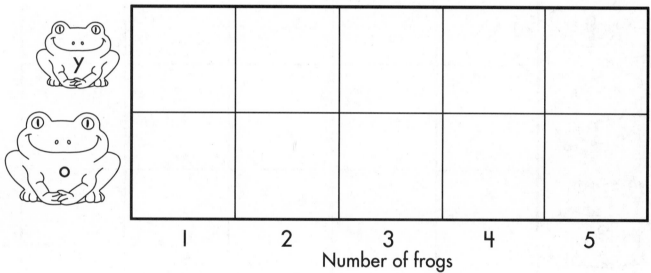

Number of frogs

A. How many small yellow frogs? _____

B. How many medium orange frogs? _____

C. Which group has more frogs? _____

D. How many more frogs? _____

Use Frog House and
small and medium frogs.
Record your work.

Name _____

Match the frogs in Frog House.
Sort your frogs by color and size.
Start at the left side of the graph.
Put each frog on the graph where it belongs.

Color the graph to record.

Frog House Frogs

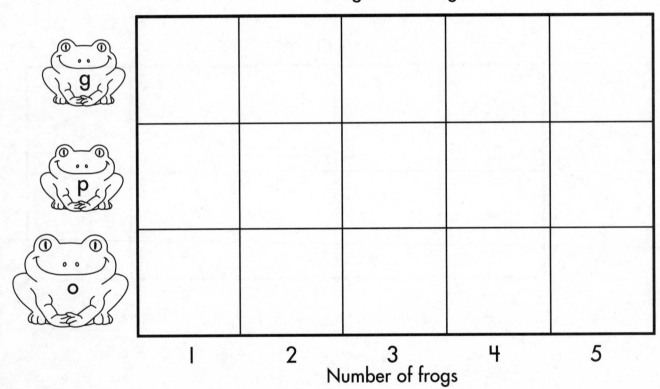

Number of frogs

A. How many small green frogs? _____

B. How many small purple frogs? _____

C. How many medium orange frogs? _____

D. Which group has the most frogs? _____

E. Which group has the fewest frogs? _____

ACTIVITY 18

Use Frog House and
small and medium frogs.
Record your work.

Name _____

Match the frogs in Frog House.
Sort your frogs by color and size.
Start at the left side of the graph.
Put each frog on the graph where it belongs.

Color the graph to record.

Frog House Frogs

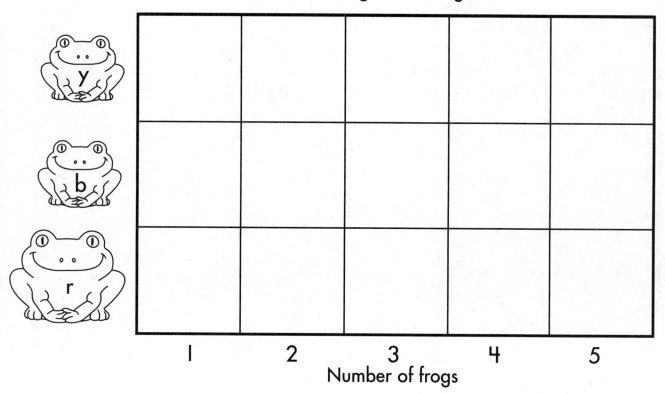

Number of frogs

A. How many small yellow frogs? _____

B. How many small blue frogs? _____

C. How many medium red frogs? _____

D. Which group has the most frogs? _____

E. Which group has the fewest frogs? _____

Use small and medium frogs.

Name _____

Match the frogs.

Use Frog Town and small and medium frogs. Record your work.

Name _____

Match the frogs in Frog Town.
Sort your frogs by color and size.
Start at the left side of the graph.
Put each frog on the graph where it belongs.

Color the graph to record.

Frog Town Frogs

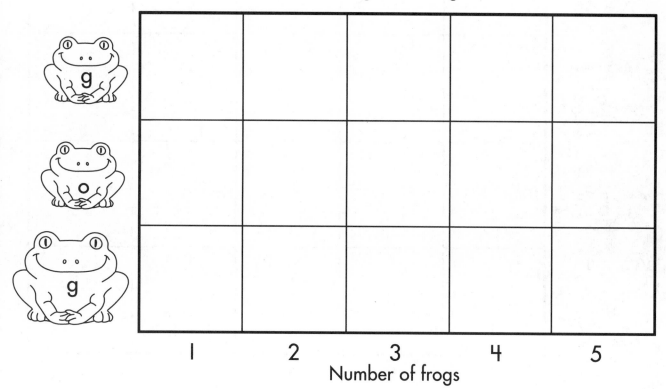

Number of frogs

A. How many small green frogs? _____

B. How many small orange frogs? _____

C. How many medium green frogs? _____

D. Which group has the most frogs? _____

ACTIVITY 21

Use Frog Town and
small and medium frogs.
Record your work.

Name _____

Match, then sort your frogs by color and size.
Color the graph to record.

Frog Town Frogs

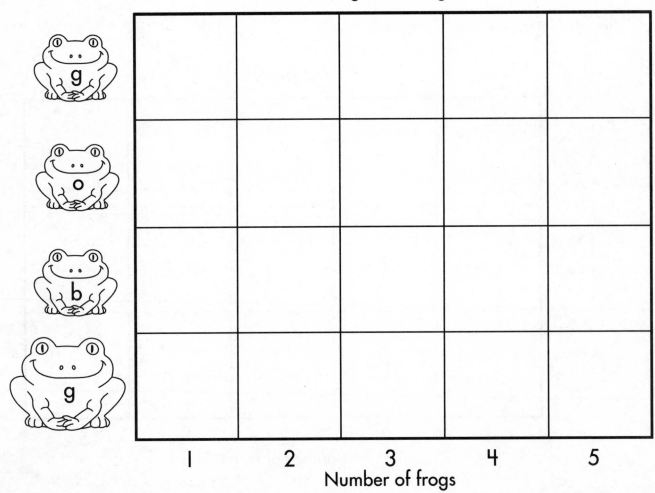

Number of frogs

A. How many small green frogs? _____

B. How many medium green frogs? _____

C. Which group has the most frogs? _____

D. Which group has the fewest frogs? _____

     0-7424-2771-4 Funtastic Frogs™ Math Volume 2

Use Frog Town and
small and medium frogs.
Record your work.

Name _____

Match, then sort your frogs by color and size.
Color the graph to record.

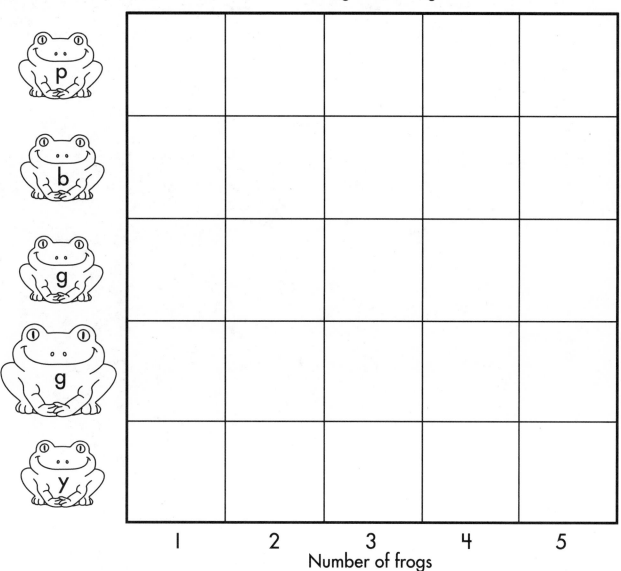

Frog Town Frogs

Number of frogs

A. Which group has the most frogs? _____

B. Which group has the fewest frogs? _____

C. Which groups have the same number of frogs? _____

Funtastic FROGS™

Beginning
Problem Solving

Unit V

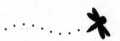

Teacher's Notes for This Unit

In Unit V, *Beginning Problem Solving,* children use the frog counters to:
- sort and match objects according to color and size
- move and manipulate concrete objects
- recognize and continue patterns
- use objects to act out a problem
- use a picture or diagram to clarify thinking
- use patterns to make predictions
- use logical reasoning and language
- reason about numbers

The activities in this unit are designed to teach strategies for solving different types of problems. The skills developed in matching, sorting, classifying, patterning, and organizing data help children develop the ability to reason and will lay the foundation for higher-level mathematics in later years. All the activities in this unit support current mathematics standards.

Contents

This unit contains 24 activities divided into four sections. Each section contains similar types of activities, giving children the opportunity to practice and use each problem-solving strategy. The unit also includes activities where children may choose a problem-solving strategy.

Solutions are provided on page 135. A photocopy master for the frog counters is also included on page 136.

Math Skills and Understandings	Related Activities
Use concrete objects	Activities 1–24
Match objects according to color and size	Activities 1–4, 6–8, 10–15, 17–19, 21–24
Recognize and continue a pattern	Activities 1–5, 22
Act out problems using objects	Activities 6–10, 23
Use the language of reasoning	Activities 6–10, 21
Use logical reasoning	Activities 16–20, 21
Make a picture or a diagram	Activities 11–15, 24
Make predictions	Activities 3, 4, 5, 22
Reason about numbers	Activities 9, 10, 15, 18, 23

Suggestions for Classroom Use

Encourage children to share their thinking with the whole class. Talking about their thinking helps children clarify their thoughts and allows others to hear how they might solve the same problem a different way. Talking about how they solve problems helps children make mathematical connections and deepens their understanding. Class discussions encourage the type of thinking required for reasoning and problem solving.

Materials

You may wish to make an overhead transparency of the first activity page in each section as an introduction to the activities that follow.

For each child, pair of children, or group, you will need:
- pencils
- crayons or colored markers to match the colors of the frogs
- a tub of frogs in three sizes and six colors
- an activity sheet for each child or pair of children

Introducing the Activities

This exploration prior to beginning the activities provides an opportunity to introduce vocabulary used throughout the unit. Introduce terms such as *first, altogether, ahead, middle,* and *last* informally. Use the terms that are appropriate for your children's age level. It is also a good time to introduce the symbols that will appear on some activity pages. The frogs' sizes are referred to as *small, medium,* and *large.* The color for each frog is represented by the first letter of each color word on the chest of the frog. Be sure all pupils are familiar with these terms before you begin instruction.

red   blue   yellow   green   purple   orange

When you introduce a section of the unit, lead the children through the first activity in that section. Discuss the directions and how to record their work. You may wish to discuss the strategy they will use to solve that problem, for example, look for a pattern. When reviewing an activity with the group, encourage the children to talk about their discoveries. This will help them make connections and clarify their thinking.

Mathematical Content by Section

Activities 1–5: Look for a pattern. Be sure children understand what a pattern is—an arrangement that repeats in a logical way. This is a good time to ask children questions such as: *What do you think comes next? Why? How do you know?*

Activities 6–10: Act out with objects. All the activities in this book incorporate this technique of problem solving; however these particular problems require more manipulation of objects than the others. Again, in this section, the language of reasoning is important, as you ask children: *What does ahead mean? What does back mean?*

Activities 11–15: Make a picture or a diagram. Often drawing a picture helps clarify information that may not be seen readily. In Activities 11 and 12 the children may move a frog counter along the path or paths they choose, and then draw in the lines with a pencil or crayon. Activities 13–15 involve patterns, but drawing a picture is probably an easier problem-solving method for young children.

Activities 16–20: Use logical reasoning. Children are introduced to the language of reasoning and will encounter terms such as *not, more than,* and *fewer than* in solving these problems. Encourage the children to move the frog counters about in working on these problems and to discuss procedures and possible solutions with each other. Ask questions such as: *Why is the answer not this frog?* in Activities 16 and 17. For Activity 18, make it clear that each frog may eat only one thing, so the children might want to discuss their reasoning. In Activity 20, there are two rules the children must keep in mind: seven frogs get on the boat, and there are two colors of counters.

Activities 21–24: Choose a strategy. Children may solve these problems by using one of the strategies they have learned. In the Solution section one strategy is named, but any strategy that works is perfectly acceptable. In Activity 24, explain that there are several ways for Blue Frog to reach the swamp. She can go out her gate or over the fence. She can then go either past trees, grass, or a log. Help the children visualize all the possibilities.

Sample Solutions for This Unit

These are sample solutions. Additional solutions are possible for some activities.

Activity

1 blue, yellow, blue, yellow

2 yellow; yellow; yellow, red

3 purple

4 green

5A. 4 **5B.** 10

6 yellow

7 sixth lily pad (next to last)

8 11 frogs: 1 red, 2 orange, 1 green, 1 blue, 2 yellow, 4 purple

9 4 frogs

10 purple, first; blue, second; yellow, third; orange, last

11  **12**

13 6 ropes

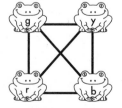

Activity

14 step 1: Orange Frog, step 2: Green Frog, step 3: Yellow Frog, step 4: Blue Frog

15 16 feet

16 large blue frog

17 large orange frog

18 Yellow Frog: bug; Green Frog: candy bar; Purple Frog: lollipop

19A. 6 frogs   **19B.** 6

20 3 blue and 4 yellow frogs (Act out with objects)

21

22 7 red frogs

23B. 3 frogs   **23C.** 2 frogs

24A.   **24B.** 6 ways

Name _____

Use small frogs.
Record your work.

Match the frogs.
Continue the pattern.
Color to record.

b

y

b

y

b

y

Use small and
medium frogs.
Record your work.

Name _____

Match the frogs.
Look for a pattern.
What colors are missing?
Color to record.

Use medium frogs.
Record your work.

Name _____

Match the frogs.
Color and continue the pattern.
What color would the 12th frog be?

Use small, medium,
and large frogs.
Record your work.

Name _____

Match the frogs.
Color and continue the pattern.
What color will the 9th frog be?

Use small frogs.
Record your work.

Name _____

Match each frog.

A. Put frogs in the bank.
This is how they go in.

At 1 o'clock, 1 frog goes in.
At 2 o'clock, 2 frogs go in.
At 3 o'clock, 3 frogs go in.

If frogs keep going in the
same way, how many frogs
will go at 4 o'clock?

Write the number._____

B. How many frogs altogether
will be in the bank at
4 o'clock?

Write the number._____

Use small frogs.
Record your work.

Name _____

Four frogs line up for lunch.
Red Frog is first in line.
Blue Frog is in front of Yellow Frog.
Green Frog is in front of Blue Frog.
What color is the last frog in line?

Color the frogs to show your answer.

**Use one medium frog.
Record your work.**

Name _____

Orange Frog wants to hop.
First, he hops to the next lily pad.
Then he hops ahead 2 more pads.
He goes back 1 pad.
Then he hops ahead 3 pads.

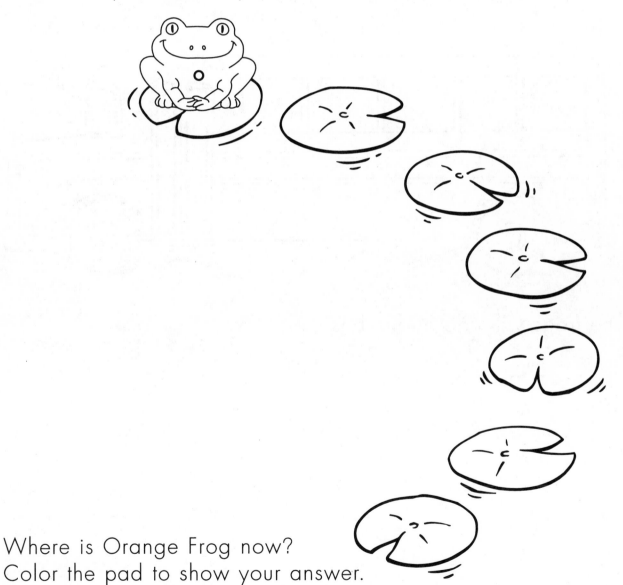

Where is Orange Frog now?
Color the pad to show your answer.

Use small frogs.
Record your work.

Name _____

Match the frogs.

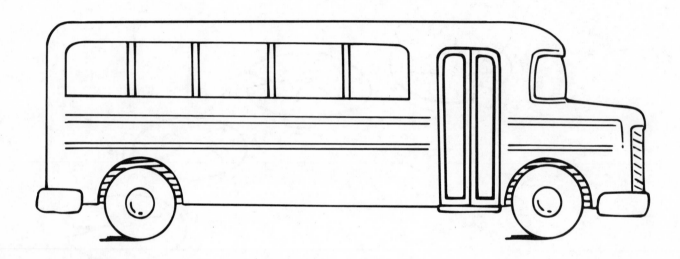

The frogs will ride on the bus.

Red Frog takes 2 orange friends.
Green Frog takes 1 blue friend.
Yellow Frogs each take 2 purple friends.
Put the frogs and their friends on the bus.
How many frogs in all are on the bus?

Write the number. _____

Use small, medium, and large frogs. Record your work.

Name _____

Match the frogs.

Move the frogs.
Small frogs go to school.
Medium frogs go to the store.
Large frogs go to the pool.
How many frogs go to school?

Write the number. _____

ACTIVITY 10

Use medium frogs.
Record your work.

Name _____

Four frogs are running a race.

Orange Frog is not first.
Purple Frog is in front of Blue Frog.
Yellow Frog is third.
Blue Frog is not last.

Put the frogs in order.
Color to record.

 first

 second

 third

 last

ACTIVITY 11

Use one small frog.
Record your work.

Name _____

Match and color Green Frog.

She is going to the pond.
Show her the way.
Draw a line.

Match and color Purple Frog.

He is going swimming. The line shows 1 way he can go.
Draw lines to show the 3 other ways.

Match and color the frogs.

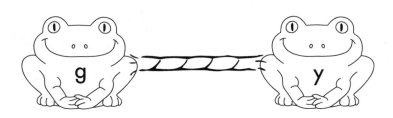

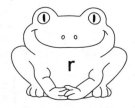 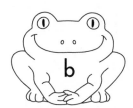

The frog friends are walking.
They want to stay together.
Each frog holds a rope to each other frog.
Show the other 5 ropes.
How many ropes in all?

Write the number. _____

Use small frogs.
Record your work.

Name _____

Red Frog sees her friends on the steps.
She hops up 4 steps to talk to Blue Frog.
Then she hops down 3 steps to talk to Orange Frog.
Next, she hops up 2 steps to talk to Yellow Frog.
Then she hops down 1 step to talk to Green Frog.

Color each frog to match the story.

Match and color the frogs.

Each frog has 1 head.
Each frog has 4 feet.
Draw the feet on each frog.
How many feet in all?

Write the number._____

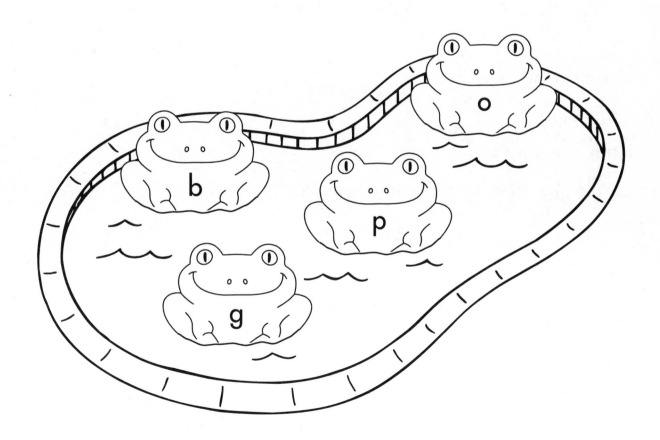

Use logical reasoning

ACTIVITY 16

Name _____

Use small, medium,
and large frogs.
Record your work.

Match and color the frogs.

Which frog am I?

I am blue.

I am not small.

Circle the frog to show the answer.

Use small, medium, and large frogs. Record your work.

Name _____

Match and color the frogs.

Which frog am I?

I am not red.

I am large.

I am not yellow.

Circle the frog to show the answer.

Use medium frogs.
Record your work.

Name _____

A. Match and color the frogs.

Yellow Frog eats bugs.
Green Frog eats sweets.
Purple Frog eats round things.

Show what each frog eats.
Draw 1 line from each frog to a picture.

Use medium frogs.
Record your work.

Name _____

A. Put frogs on the .

There are more than 4 frogs.
There are fewer than 8 frogs.
There is an even number of frogs.

B. How many frogs are on the ?

Make an X for each frog.

Write the number. _____

Use small frogs.
Record your work.

Name _____

Match the frogs.

Only seven frogs can get on the boat.
There can only be two colors.
Put the frogs on the boat.
Color to record.

ACTIVITY 21

**Use one small frog.
Record your work.**

Name _____

Match and color Yellow Frog.

She wants a new hat.
She likes dots.
She likes flowers.
She does not like bows.

Color the hat Yellow Frog wants.

Use small frogs.
Record your work.

Name _____

Match the frogs.
They are going for a boat ride.

One frog rides
in the first boat.

Three frogs ride
in the second boat.

Five frogs ride
in the third boat.

How many red frogs would ride in the fourth boat?

Write the number._____

Use small frogs.
Record your work.

Name _____

A. Match the frogs.
They are at the beach.

B. The frogs will ride
in 2 boats.
The same number of frogs
will ride in each boat.
How many frogs in each boat?

Write the number. _____

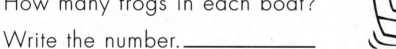

C. Then the frogs will sit
on 3 rafts.
The same number of
frogs will sit on each raft.
How many frogs on
each raft?

Write the number. _____

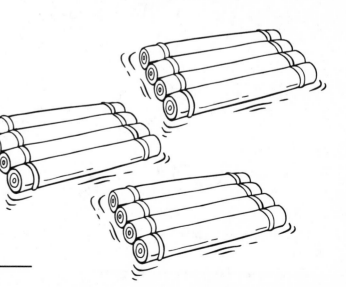

Use one small frog.
Record your work.

Name _____

A. Match and color Blue Frog.
   She wants to go to the swamp.
   She can go out the gate or over the fence.
   She can go by the trees, the grass, or the log.
   Draw a line to show each way to the swamp.

B. How many ways to the swamp?

   Write the number. _____